The Fatimids

2. The Rule from Egypt

Shainool Jiwa

I.B. TAURIS

LONDON · NEW YORK · OXFORD · NEW DELHI · SYDNEY

In association with
The Institute of Ismaili Studies
LONDON

I.B. TAURIS
Bloomsbury Publishing Plc
50 Bedford Square, London, WC1B 3DP, UK
1385 Broadway, New York, NY 10018, USA
29 Earlsfort Terrace, Dublin 2, Ireland

In association with The Institute of Ismaili Studies
Aga Khan Centre, 10 Handyside Street, London N1C 4DN
www.iis.ac.uk

BLOOMSBURY, I.B. TAURIS and the I.B. Tauris logo are trade-
marks of Bloomsbury Publishing Plc

First published in Great Britain 2023

A catalogue record for this book is available from the
British Library.

A catalog record for this book is available from the Library
of Congress.

ISBN: PB: 978-1-7807-6948-6
       ePDF: 978-0-7556-4675-3
       eBook: 978-0-7556-4676-0

Series: World of Islam

Typeset by RefineCatch Limited, Bungay, Suffolk
Printed and bound in Great Britain

To find out more about our authors and books visit
www.bloomsbury.com and sign up for our newsletters.

Contents

Acknowledgements

This second volume on the Fatimids has richly benefited from several colleagues at the IIS: Dr Hasan al-Khoee, Tara Woolnough, Lisa Morgan, Russell Harris, and Sarah Campbell, who have shepherded the text through various stages of its production. My sincere gratitude to Dr Shiraz Kabani for a lifetime of friendship and support. Shahnavaz, Adil, and Nabila – you are the beacons of my life.

Note on the Text

In the interest of readability, notes have been kept to a minimum, with primary-source quotes referenced in the endnotes. Similarly, diacritics for transliterated words have been limited to the *ayn* (ʿ) and the *hamza* (ʾ) where they occur in the middle of a word. The words *ibn* and *bint* meaning 'son of' and 'daughter of' respectively are abbreviated to b. and bt. when occurring in the middle of a name. All dates are Common Era, unless otherwise indicated. Supplementary material related to the content of the book is available on the IIS website: www.iis.ac.uk

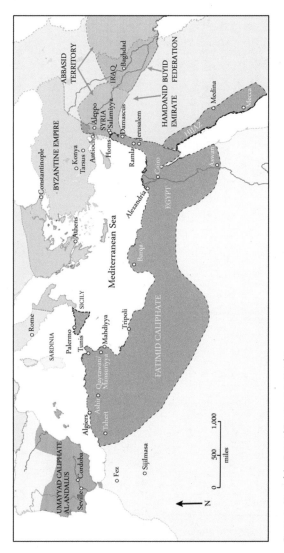

Figure 1. Map of the Fatimid Empire at its Height

Introduction

There are moments in history when the past, the present, and the future seem to clash at an accelerated pace, as if fired through a hadron collider, resulting in epochal changes in human civilization. Such significant events – whether the onset of the First and Second World Wars, the independence movements in Asia and Africa, or the collapse of the Soviet Union – were understood as being transformative by those who lived through them, long before later historians pronounced their judgement.

In the few years that have elapsed between the publication of *The Fatimids: 1. The Rise of a Muslim Empire* and this second volume, much in the world has been irrevocably transformed. Amidst fractious social, economic, and political convulsions, humankind has witnessed tangible signs of its wilful neglect of the environment and has faced a stark reminder of its own fragility in the face of a global pandemic.

Through all such epochal transformations, one distinct feature of the human experience remains constant: our inclination to look to the past to make meaning of the present. This impetus animated the Greek historians of the third century BCE just as it did the Church fathers between the first and eighth centuries. It galvanized pioneers of Muslim historical literature in the 9th and 10th centuries and their successors in the medieval period, and it animated the works of early modern historians of 18th- and 19th-century Europe. Today, it shapes both popular and academic history writing, including this book.

The establishment of the Fatimid caliphate in the 10th century was arguably one such moment of significant transformation in the medieval Muslim world. This is attested by the indelible imprint it made on Islamic history, thought, literature, art, architecture, and aesthetics over the two-and-a-half centuries of its existence (909 to 1171). The period continues to elicit significant interest across various disciplinary fields to this day.

Led by a hereditary succession of Imams (authoritative religious guides), the Fatimids proclaimed their descent from the Prophet Muhammad (d. 632) through his eldest daughter Fatima (d. 632) and his cousin and son-in-law, Ali b. Abi Talib (d. 661). The Fatimids' religious and political authority was manifested in their establishment of the first Ismaili Shi'i caliphate to rule over the heartlands of the Muslim world. From 909 to 973 – the subject of volume 1 of this work – Fatimid rule was centred in North Africa and along the Mediterranean littoral. From 973 to 1171 – the focus of this volume – the Fatimid caliphate evolved from a provincial dynasty in North Africa to a thriving Mediterranean Empire centred in Egypt. Their settlement in the country transformed Egypt from what had already been a lucrative regional province under previous administrations to the capital hub of an empire for the first time in a millennium.

During this second phase of their history, the Fatimids founded Cairo and oversaw its development into a major cultural and economic nexus linking Asia, Africa, and Europe. The empire's affluence engendered a vibrant cultural, artistic, and intellectual milieu, reflecting the broader civilizational élan of the age. The Fatimids marshalled significant developments in statecraft and civic life. However, they also had to contend with political and ideological rivalries from the neighbouring Abbasid, Umayyad, and Byzantine Empires, as well as the challenges of governing a multi-ethnic populace consisting of multi-denominational communities from the Muslim, Christian, and Jewish faiths. They weathered these challenges by developing inclusive approaches to governance, administration, and the judiciary, which allowed for the largely peaceful co-existence of communities within their realms. The Fatimids also patronized public ceremonials that venerated the Prophet and his family (his *ahl al-bayt*); these commemorations remain a feature of devotional practice in many Muslim societies today.

The formation of the Fatimid caliphate also marks a watershed in the religious history of the Muslim world, particularly in the history of the Ismaili Shiʿi community. For the Ismailis, the Fatimid Imam-caliphs were part of a continuum of divinely designated Imams descended from the family of the Prophet Muhammad. In Ismaili Shiʻi doctrine, the imamate began when the Prophet – in 632, at Ghadir Khumm, shortly before his demise – declared his cousin and son-in-law Ali b. Abi Talib the first Imam. The Nizari Ismailis believe the succession of Imams in direct descent from Imam Ali and Hazrat Fatima continued from the seventh century, through to the Fatimid Imam-caliphs, and on into the present day to the 49th Imam-of-the-Time, Shah Karim al-Husayni (b. 1936). Today, the Ismailis are the second largest community of Shiʻi Muslims, after the Ithnaʻasharis, and they reside across the Middle East, South and Central Asia, East and South Africa, as well as in Europe, Canada, and the United States.

An important concept in early Muslim intellectual traditions centred on the idea of the turning of time. This was encapsulated in the Arabic term *dawla* – literally the turning of a cycle – which, having been used to denote the successful alternation between one ruling power and another, came by the 10th century to denote a dynastic state. The use of *dawla* to mean a government remains widely used in the Arab world today. For many medieval Muslim writers, the Fatimid *dawla* was thus a new turn in the political history of the region, whose era replaced that of earlier *dawla*s. The Fatimids themselves conceived of their polity as the *dawlat al-haqq* – the 'rightly guided state' – in which principles of legitimate authority and justice were to underpin their governance over the Muslim world. In our

21st-century era of turns and transformations, the history of the Fatimids provides a reading of how past communities developed creative responses to the rhythms of continuity and change in human society.

Presenting a comprehensive account of over two centuries of complex and dynamic Fatimid rule in Egypt in a slim volume is a tall order. However, the book aims to provide the major contours, figures, and developments that shaped the course of the Fatimid age in Egypt, thus enabling non-specialist readers to develop an understanding of this critical era of Muslim and Mediterranean history.

Fatimid studies is a burgeoning field of scholarship. The wide-ranging discovery of sources and artefacts – from primary texts, cartographies, and archaeological findings to fragments of the Cairo *geniza* – continues to invigorate the field today. For those readers enticed to further explore the subject, select recommended reads are provided at the end of the book.

Conventionally, coverage of the Fatimids ends in 1171, the final year in which the Fatimid Imam-caliph's name was pronounced in Egypt's mosques. While periodization and geographic spatialization are necessary for a sound historical survey, they can sometimes impose limitations on studies of the past, and Fatimid history has tended to suffer from this. Not only is the Fatimid era in Egypt often divorced from its North-African antecedent, but coverage of the broader history of the empire is often restricted to the geographical confines of Egypt. Across Fatimid history, Ismaili followers of the Imam-caliphs lived in communities as far afield as Yemen, Sindh, Iran, and Central Asia. With their religious leadership located in the Imam-caliphs of Cairo, developments in the Fatimid Empire shaped the distinct trajectories of these communities.

Today, the Nizaris and the Tayyibis are the principal representatives of the Ismaili Shi'i tradition. Both emerged from communities of the Fatimid *da'wa* in Iran and Yemen respectively in the final century of the Fatimid age, and both charted their identities and doctrinal markers following developments in Cairo. Consequently, to understand the scope, impact, and legacy of the Fatimids, a wide-angled historical lens is required – one which includes not only Egypt, but the wider Muslim world.

Fatimid Rulers in Ifriqiya and Egypt 909–1171

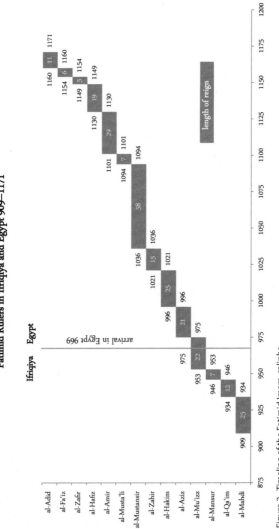

Figure 2. Timeline of the Fatimid Imam-caliphs

Chapter 1

The Arrival of the Fatimids in Egypt

On Tuesday, 11 June 973, as the sun rose over the lush Nile valley, the people of Egypt awoke to witness a momentous event. Years of preparations had reached their crescendo. In Fustat, the old capital of Egypt that sat astride the Nile, decorations adorned the city. Over the river itself, new pontoon bridges had been built in anticipation. But the grandest of preparations was underway a few kilometres north where for four years, builders, architects, craftsmen, and artisans had constructed a new royal city. There, a new palace and mosque had been built, and residential areas had been laid out – all surrounded by four large walls with towering gates. Awaiting its inauguration, it would soon be named *al-Qahira al-Muʿizziya* (the City Victorious of al-Muʿizz). In time this would be shortened to *al-Qahira* (Cairo, as it continues to be known today).

On the other side of the river, on the plains of Giza that for millennia had been flanked by the ancient pyramids, the new ruler of Egypt – the Imam-caliph al-Muʿizz li-Din Allah (d. 975) – appeared riding regally on horseback. Preceded by a procession of people on foot, al-Muʿizz crossed the river, alighting on its eastern bank. Riding northwards, he entered Cairo for the very first time. In his palace, he fell to the ground prostrating in gratitude to God.

A grand retinue had accompanied al-Muʿizz in his journey to Egypt. The Imam-caliph had also brought with him three coffins: those of his father, grandfather, and great-grandfather, the first three Imam-caliphs of the Fatimid realms. They were soon reinterred in a sanctified wing of the palace which came to be known as the Saffron Tomb (*Turbat al-Zaʿfaran*). While al-Muʿizz's journey to Egypt had taken just over a year, that of his predecessors in reaching this juncture had taken over six decades.

The Fatimids in North Africa

The Fatimid Empire was founded in 909 in Ifriqiya (a region encompassing Tunisia and eastern Algeria today).[1] There, in the Great Mosque of Qayrawan, the Ismaili Shiʿi Imam Abd Allah al-Mahdi bi'llah (d. 934) had been proclaimed the *amir al-muʾminin* (commander of the faithful), a declaration that pronounced him as the sole righteous Imam and caliph over the Muslim world. In his 25-year rule, al-Mahdi oversaw the genesis of the Fatimid state. Initially he reigned from the palace town of Raqqada, but in 921 al-Mahdi inaugurated the first newly built Fatimid capital city, called al-Mahdiyya, on the Mediterranean coast.

Al-Muʿizz was born at al-Mahdiyya in 931, during the final years of his great-grandfather al-Mahdi's reign. While growing up, he witnessed

the turbulence that erupted during the early years
of Fatimid rule. As a young boy, during the reign
of his grandfather, the second Fatimid Imam-
caliph al-Qa'im bi Amr Allah (d. 946), al-Mu'izz
experienced the Khariji anti-Fatimid rebellion that
began in 943 and shook the foundations of Fatimid
rule. When al-Qa'im passed away in 946 at the
height of the rebellion, al-Mu'izz then saw up
close the tribulations of the reign of his own father,
al-Mansur bi'llah (d. 953). Taking often to the
battlefield, al-Mansur ended the rebellion by
947, and he spent the following years enacting
policies to reverse the depredations of war by
restoring the local economy and people's liveli-
hoods. Al-Mansur's victory was architecturally
commemorated with the building of a second
Fatimid city, al-Mansuriyya, located a few kilometres south of Qayrawan – historically a
heartland of Sunni scholarship. The positioning
of the new Fatimid city and the appointment of
a Maliki Sunni governor over Qayrawan became
major milestones in the evolution of Fatimid
governance, signalling greater inclusivity of different elements of North-African society within the
Shi'i caliphate.

On the passing of al-Mansur in 953, al-Mu'izz,
aged 22 and whose birthname was Ma'add, was
proclaimed the fourth Fatimid Imam-caliph with
the regnal title *al-Mu'izz li-Din Allah* (the Glorifier
of the Religion of God). The first decade of his reign
was spent consolidating Fatimid control in the
region. By then, the Fatimid Empire encompassed
present-day Tunisia, Algeria, and parts of Morocco,

as well Libya, Cyrenaica, and the island of Sicily. Its lands were inhabited by people of diverse ethnicities – Arabs, Berbers, Greeks, and Turks, among others – and of varied denominations from the Muslim, Christian, and Jewish faiths.

The complexities of managing diverse multitudes, and the periodic challenges arising from Maliki Arab and Khariji Berber leaders opposed to a Shi'i caliphate, occupied the first Fatimid Imam-caliphs for much of the initial six decades. Nonetheless, the experience of statecraft proved invaluable, and the precedents then established became some of the hallmarks of Fatimid rule in Egypt. At the core of the Fatimids' model of governance, however, lay the cardinal Shi'i principle of the imamate, which had animated the establishment of their state.

The Imamate and the Origins of the Fatimid Caliphate

The origins of the Fatimid Empire lay in a ninth-century movement whose *raison d'etre* was defined by its response to questions that had arisen in the first decades of Muslim history. Following the Prophet Muhammad's death in 632, the nascent Muslim community (*umma*) diverged in its responses to the identity and role of the Prophet's successor. Over time, the varied viewpoints regarding religious guidance and political authority gave rise to several religious and legal schools of Islam.

Caliphs (from the Arabic *khalifa*, meaning deputy or representative) from among the companions of the Prophet first ruled over the *umma* from

632 to 661. They were followed by caliphs of the Umayyad caliphate in Syria (661–750), then of the Abbasid caliphate in Iraq (750–1258). Each ruler upheld the claim to universal authority over the *umma*. Throughout the first centuries, however, disputes among the various Muslim communities regarding succession and religious leadership often led to periods of civil war and oppression.

Among the earliest Muslims were those who maintained that the Prophet's authority continued only in his immediate family. Known today as the Shi'a, they held that *imam*s (religio-political leaders) from the household of the Prophet (*ahl al-bayt*) had been appointed by God to succeed the Prophet, the first of whom was his cousin, the Imam Ali b. Abi Talib. Thereafter, many of these supporters of Ali (*shi'at Ali*, whence the term Shi'a is derived) regarded the imamate as being exclusively inherited by al-Hasan and al-Husayn – the sons of Ali and Fatima – and thereafter through their designated male descendants.

As branches of the Shi'a emerged in the eighth century, the Imamis – to which the Ismaili and Ithna'ashari (Twelver) Shi'a belong – explicated doctrines concerning legitimate leadership. Imami Shi'ism holds that the Imams from the Prophet's descendants are appointed by God as successors to the Prophet's religious and political authority. As recipients of divinely inspired knowledge (*ilm*), they are the sole designated leaders of the *umma*, the true guides to God's path, and the chosen mediums of salvation. The line of Imams is deemed to have continued in Imam al-Husayn's male descent, with each Imam explicitly appointing his successor according to God's decree (*nass*). Following the demise of Imam Ja'far al-Sadiq in 765, the Imami Shi'a branched further, with the Ismaili Shi'a tracing the line of Imams through his eldest son, Ismail.

The same period also saw the gradual emergence of the Sunni traditions, so defined by their proclaimed adherence to the *sunna* (precedent) and traditions of the Prophet Muhammad. The nascent Sunni schools of law were largely supportive of the political authority of the Abbasid caliphs. They maintained, however, that religious authority was vested in their own scholars (*ulama*), stemming from their knowledge (*ilm*) of the traditions of the Prophet Muhammad and religious law.

The Shi'a had long suffered persecution under Umayyad and Abbasid rule. By the mid-800s, however, the once powerful Abbasid Empire was on the wane, and by the 900s, its political power had fragmented, with local dynasties and rival military governors ruling different provinces. This collapse of Abbasid authority facilitated the proliferation of numerous Shi'i movements, such that the 10th century would be labelled the 'Shi'i century'.

The Da'wa and the End of Concealment

It was in this milieu that Ismaili Shi'i movements gained momentum. According to the post-10th-century Ismaili tradition, for almost a century-and-a-half (765–909), in what came to be called the period of concealment (*dawr al-satr*), the Ismailis had kept the identity of their Imams concealed, to stave off the imminent Abbasid threat. By the mid-ninth century, however, the Ismaili Imams – who were then based in Salamiyya, Syria – had emerged as leaders of a hierarchical organization known as the *da'wa* (the calling). From within the organization, Ismaili emissaries (*da'is*) appeared in Central Asia, Iran, Iraq, Syria, the Arabian Peninsula, Yemen, Egypt, and North Africa, summoning allegiance to the Ismaili Imam. They pronounced that the divinely appointed Imam would restore justice and establish the rightly guided state (*dawlat al-haqq*) based on his authoritative knowledge of the true religion (*din al-haqq*).

Ifriqiya was among the regions where the *da'wa* found receptivity. There, in the late 800s, Berber tribes known as the Kutama joined the Ismaili movement in large numbers. Under the leadership of the Ismaili *da'i* Abu Abd Allah al-Shi'i (d. 911), they gathered in newly fortified towns and prepared for an inevitable showdown with the Aghlabids (800–909), who ruled the region as Abbasid viceroys. Following a decade of military engagement, Abu Abd Allah's forces entered Qayrawan. Soon thereafter, in January 910, the Ismaili Imam Abd Allah al-Mahdi bi'llah was publicly proclaimed the first Fatimid Imam-caliph. Just over 60 years later, al-Mu'izz's entry into Egypt marked the beginning of the Egyptian phase of Fatimid history.

The Entry into Egypt

Fatimid interest in Egypt, a country where the *daʿwa* had laid deep roots, had been longstanding. Between 913 and 925, three Fatimid expeditions had sought to wrest the country from Abbasid control but met little success. From 935, Egypt had been ruled by the Ikhshidids, a dynasty of Turkish governors who pledged nominal allegiance to the Abbasids. In 966, however, their powerful regent, Kafur al-Ikhshidi, passed away. In the ensuing void, civil war and strife became rife, crime and brigandage escalated, and trade ground to a halt. The Ismaili *daʿwa* gained a renewed potency, and Egypt's leading figures wrote to the Fatimid al-Muʿizz asking him to extend his rule over the country.

Preparations for a Fatimid expedition thus began in earnest. By February 968, al-Muʿizz's leading general, Jawhar al-Siqilli, or al-Saqlabi, left Ifriqiya at the head of a grand army and marched eastwards. Fifteen months later, in May 969, the famed white banners of the Fatimid caliphate were fluttering by the Nile.

The Aman *Declaration*

The Fatimid entry was largely peaceful. Soon after his arrival, the general Jawhar encamped near Alexandria where he received a delegation of Egyptian notables which included the chief minister of the previous Ikhshidid government. However, the group was led by Abu Jaʿfar Muslim al-Husayni, a leader of Egypt's *ashraf* (nobles). Then, this appellation referred to all the living descendants of the Prophet Muhammad who, numbering in their thousands, held a distinct status across the Muslim world. Thus, in choosing Abu Ja'far Muslim to lead the negotiations, the Egyptians drew on the *sharif*'s kinship with the Fatimid Imam-caliphs.

The meeting resulted in the issuance of a famous document on behalf of al-Mu'izz that would come to constitute the blueprint of Fatimid governance in Egypt. Known as an *aman* (guarantee of safety), it was read out in Egypt's capital Fustat by the *sharif* Abu Ja'far Muslim. Proclaiming the sovereignty of the Fatimid Imam-caliph over the Muslim world, it enunciated the principles of governance that would underpin the Fatimid Imam-caliph's authority. The *aman* above all pledged a guarantee of safety and security to all the inhabitants of Egypt – Muslims, Christians, and Jews. It pledged the commitment to defend the frontiers from Byzantine incursions, restore the *hajj* (pilgrimage) – which had been suspended for several years – annul illegal taxes, protect traders from brigandage, and ameliorate the economy. Building on the precedent of al-Mansur, the *aman* of al-Mu'izz also assured Sunni Muslims of the continuation of their religious practices, encapsulated in the promise, 'You shall continue in your *madhhab* [school of law].'[2]

After brief skirmishes with remnants of the Ikhshidid army, Jawhar rode south to Giza on 5 July 969, then continued to the intended site of the new capital city. There, as commanded by the Imam-caliph, he issued the order for the construction of Cairo. 'When the Egyptians came to congratulate him in the morning, they found that he had dug the foundations of the palace through the night.'[3]

Over the next four years, Jawhar established Fatimid rule in Egypt. New administrators were appointed, coinage and market practices were reformed, and security measures were introduced. In the weekly Friday *khutbas* (sermons), the Shi'i doctrines that underpinned Fatimid rule – and the reverence for the *ahl al-bayt* – were pronounced.

Securing Egypt's eastern border was a foremost priority. In Palestine and Syria, remnants of the Ikhshidid dynasty allied with local forces to resist the Fatimid advance. By 970, a Fatimid army led by a noted Kutama Berber general, Ja'far b. Falah, took control of Ramla and Damascus. But the expedition soon suffered severe reversals after Ja'far was killed in battle, exposing Cairo to attack. Jawhar's armies in Egypt held firm, however, and the construction of Cairo continued apace.

The Migration of the Imam and the Transfer of State

When news first reached Ifriqiya of Jawhar's success, the Fatimid capital al-Mansuriyya (in modern Tunisia) erupted in celebration. This soon gave way to industrious endeavour, as al-Mu'izz decreed a momentous undertaking: the entire Fatimid court and government was to relocate to Egypt. The long road from Ifriqiya to Egypt was equipped to handle the mass movement of people – roads were repaired, new wells were dug, fortresses were built, and caravansaries were restored. Meanwhile in the capital, travel documents were issued, packhorses and camels were organized, ships were built and loaded, and the contents of the Fatimid treasury were readied for transfer.

On 6 August 972, al-Muʿizz bid farewell to Ifriqiya and set out for Cairo. Thousands followed, including the entire Fatimid household as well as judges, administrators, scholars, merchants, poets, and many of the Kutama Berber tribesmen attached to the Ismaili *daʿwa*. Among them were members of al-Muʿizz's family who would become famous for their contributions in Egypt: his consort Durzan Taghrid, who would become a patron of civic and religious buildings; his eldest son Tamim, who would become a renowned poet; his second son Abd Allah, who would gain fame for his valour on the battlefield, before his untimely demise; and his third son, Nizar, who in three short years would succeed his father to the Fatimid caliphate with the regnal title *al-Aziz bi'llah* (the Glorious by God). Also among al-Muʿizz's entourage were leading Ismaili scholars of the state, the most famous being the chief *daʿi* and judge, Qadi Abu Hanifa al-Nuʿman (d. 974).

On 29 May 973, al-Muʿizz and his retinue arrived at Alexandria, where a grand reception of Egyptian notables awaited. From there, the Imam-caliph travelled southwards to Cairo. His entry into the new royal city marked a moment-ous turn in the history of both the Fatimids and

Egypt. Centuries later, one of medieval Egypt's most famous historians earmarked this occasion as a turning point when 'Egypt became the seat of a caliphate after having been the seat of an amirate.'[4]

Chapter 2

The Genesis of Fatimid Rule in Egypt

Egypt: The Gift of the Nile

For 10th-century travellers sailing along the southern shores of the Mediterranean, catching sight of the sun-blushed buildings of ancient Alexandria signalled their arrival in Egypt. Traversing inland, they would pass through the lush Nile delta. The landmarks dotting the riverbanks as they sailed further south and into Upper Egypt stood as palpable reminders of the country's millennial history.

Egypt was among the earliest cradles of civilization. From around 3100 BCE, and for the next two-and-a-half thousand years, the country was ruled by pharaohs of over thirty different dynasties, whose cities, temples, pyramids, and hieroglyphs continue to fascinate today. Then, and thereafter, many people came from near and far to make Egypt their home. In 331 BCE, Alexandria was founded by Alexander of Macedon, whose Ptolemaic successors ruled in Egypt for almost three centuries. Egypt then came under Roman rule in 30 BCE, one continued by their Byzantine inheritors, under whom pagan Egypt became predominantly Christian. In the 640s, the Muslim caliphate drew Egypt into its fold. The Muslim garrison city of Fustat was founded on the riverbank near the old Roman fortress of Babylon, and it soon became the commercial and cultural hub of the country.

By the 10th century, Egypt stood at the confluence of a burgeoning trade network that linked the Red Sea and the Indian Ocean to the Mediterranean. Along the docks of the Nile, travellers would have seen boats brimming with commodities: spices, silks, ivory, linen, fruits, vegetables, ceramics, glass, honey, sugarcane, and exquisite gold-spun fabrics. They would have heard the medley of languages of peoples of different ethnicities. Prominent amongst them were the Christian Copts, who formed a majority in the countryside and whose language grew out of the Demotic Egyptian spoken since late antiquity. Notable, too, were the Arabs, living mainly in urban centres, often descendants of Arabian tribesmen who had settled in Egypt from the seventh century onwards. The country was also home to several other communities, including many recent arrivals: Greeks, Nubians, Turks, and Berbers.

The diversity of languages reflected the diversity of religious traditions. Sunni and Shi'i Muslims lived alongside large Christian communities of Coptic, Melkite, and Nestorian persuasions. Jews had lived in Egypt for millennia, and now included Rabbanite and Qaraite denominations. Yet while the intermingling of people enriched Egypt, it also gave way to periods of confessional strife. Riots between religious communities in Alexandria in the early Roman period became famed in history, and over time, managing such diverse communities remained one of the endemic challenges of Egyptian rule.

As the travellers continued their journey, some may have intuited the famous remark by the Greek historian Herodotus that Egypt is 'the gift of the Nile'. With its mineral-rich waters originating south in the mountains of Ethiopia and the great lakes of East Africa, the northward-flowing Nile was the lifeblood of the country. Its waters enriched swathes of farmland, producing staples such as wheat and sugarcane, and income-generating crops, including flax and cotton. This rendered the country a veritable breadbasket to the world around it. While in the first century CE, much of Rome's survival depended on imports of Egypt's grain, by the 10th century, this rang true for the lands of the Hijaz in Arabia.

The fortunes of Egypt were thus perennially tied to the Nile. Each year, around June, the Nile would begin to rise. If its waters rose to an optimal height, the river would flood its banks, fill the canals built alongside it, and deposit fertile alluvial soil. Celebrations would follow. If the waters failed to rise sufficiently, farms would remain fallow, giving way to drought and hunger. Immortalized in the images of the 'seven years of plenty' and the 'seven years of famine' recounted in the accounts of Joseph in the Old Testament and the Qur'an, the alternation between plenitude and famine had long shaped Egypt's fortunes.

Just as each of the previous civilizations had left their mark on Egypt, so too had their own worldviews and fortunes been moulded by Egypt's environment. That dynamic would remain pivotal to the unfolding of Fatimid rule.

Egyptian Witnesses of a New Age

When al-Muʿizz first crossed the Nile, Egyptian scholars were poised to record the new age. Among them was Ibn Zulaq (d. 996), then in his 50s. Already one of Egypt's most prominent historians, Ibn Zulaq would soon also compose biographies of al-Muʿizz and Jawhar. While these have not survived, excerpts were reproduced by later Egyptian historians. From 969 onwards, Ibn Zulaq recorded the events he witnessed, in which he often partook. Here is an example of this, taken when he joined the congregational prayers for the Eid al-Fitr (the Festival of the Breaking of the Fast), led by the Imam-caliph al-Muʿizz:

> In every *rakʿa* [bowing] and prostration, I recited the *tasbih* [glorification of God] after him [al-Muʿizz]* more than thirty times ... This was the prayer of his forefather, Ali b. Abi Talib.[1]

Ibn Zulaq's compositions constitute part of a larger corpus of texts and documentary sources that remain indispensable for understanding Fatimid history.

The Sources on Fatimid Egypt

Like Ibn Zulaq, many living in Fatimid Egypt wrote about the era. Among them was al-Mukhtar al-Musabbihi (d. 1030), whose voluminous 13,000-folio 'History of Egypt' (*Ta'rikh Misr*) spanned Fatimid history from 978 to 1025. Others wrote at the twilight of Fatimid rule, such as Abd al-Salam b al-Tuwayr (d. 1220), who documented the final decades of the Fatimids and the rise of their successors, the Ayyubids (1171–1260).

These authors came from diverse backgrounds and had different vantage points. While Ibn Zulaq and al-Musabbihi were scholars of the Shafi'i *madhhab* (a school of law within Sunni Islam), others such as Haydara b. Muhammad b. Ibrahim (fl. 11th century) and al-Mu'ayyad fi'l-Din al-Shirazi (d. 1078) were scholars who were part of the Fatimid *da'wa*. Contemporary Christian scholars from Egypt who wrote histories of the era include the Coptic bishop Severus Ibn al-Muqaffa (d. 987) and his successors, whose works together constituted the *History of the Patriarchs of the Coptic Church of Alexandria*, while the physician Yahya b. Sa'id al-Antaki (d. 1066) recounted events from a Melkite Christian viewpoint.

Historical works form but one genre of a broader literary corpus that found expression in Fatimid Egypt; the surviving texts from other genres provide crucial insight into the ideas that permeated the empire. Amongst them are works on religious doctrine and law by Muslim, Christian, and Jewish scholars; works of Arabic literature and poetry; and those on philosophy and the natural sciences. Their authors range from leading scientists like al-Hasan b. al-Haytham

(d. ca. 1040) to prominent *da'i*s like Hamid al-Din al-Kirmani (d. 1021). Such works also include compositions by famous Fatimid bureaucrats like Ibn al-Sayrafi (d. 1147) and government officials like the 11th-century market inspector Ibn Bassam, and travelogues by people who visited Egypt, such as the *Safarnama* ('Book of Travels') of the celebrated Iranian poet and Ismaili scholar-*da'i* Nasir-i Khusraw (d. after 1070). One recently discovered and fascinating source, probably written by a figure closely associated with the Fatimid *da'wa* in the 11th century, is the *Kitab Ghara'ib al-funun wa-mulah al-uyun* ('The Book of Curiosities of the Sciences and Marvels for the Eye'). It provides a remarkable account of the universe, the world, and of the Fatimids as a maritime empire.

There are also extensive surviving documentary sources from art and architecture. Walking through historic Cairo today, visitors encounter Fatimid-era buildings, including the al-Anwar Mosque (more commonly known as the mosque of al-Hakim), the al-Aqmar Mosque, and the Gateway of Conquests (*Bab al-Futuh*). Their architectural forms and inscriptions provide a vital perspective. Ongoing archaeological works have also recovered material artefacts, including fabrics and burial shrouds, pottery, glassware, and, in recent years, a hoard of Fatimid gold coins from the Mediterranean seabed. Amongst the most significant artefacts are those of the Cairo *geniza* from the Ben Ezra synagogue in Fustat. Here, Jewish congregants from the Fatimid period onwards stored innumerable manuscript

Figure 3. Opening Page from al-Kirmani's *Kitab al-Riyad*

The *Kitab al-Riyad* was written by al-Kirmani during the latter part of the Fatimid era. In this work, al-Kirmani sought to rectify conflicting philosophies that had arisen among Ismaili *da'i*s. The work survives today as a first-hand account of key ideas circulating during Fatimid times.

fragments and documents, including books, legal petitions, receipts, and letters to distant lands. The study of the *geniza* collections reveals a world where Jews, Christians, and Muslims lived and worked side by side.

If the sources on Fatimid history are plentiful, they also present several challenges. The upheavals of the 11th and 12th centuries witnessed the mass destruction of Fatimid texts, artefacts, and libraries. Consequently, much of Fatimid history needs to be pieced together from the writings of later historians, including those of Ibn al-Athir (d. 1233), Ibn Khallikan (d. 1282), Ibn Khaldun (d. 1406), and Ibn Taghribirdi (d. 1470) among others. These later medieval works were, however, composed in milieus that were often hostile to the Fatimids and influenced by Abbasid propaganda that sought to discredit the legitimacy of the Fatimids, especially by denying their descent from the Prophet Muhammad. So, while these sources provide vital information for us today, they need to be read in their historical context.

Noteworthy amongst these medieval compilations are the writings of the erudite Egyptian historian Taqi al-Din Ahmad b. Ali al-Maqrizi (d. 1442). Although he was a Shafi'i scholar, al-Maqrizi may have been descended from the Fatimid Imam-caliphs, and in his writings about them, he adopted an empathic and nuanced viewpoint. Living in 15th-century Cairo, al-Maqrizi had access to many sources that have not survived today, and his prolific corpus is a vital source for Fatimid history. The writings of many mentioned

Figure 4. Solomon Schechter Studying *Geniza* Documents
Solomon Schechter, ca.1898 Cambridge, studying boxes of manuscripts from the Cairo *geniza*.

Figure 5. Ben Ezra Synagogue, Cairo
State documents written by Fatimid officials have been found housed in the storeroom of Ben Ezra. Today, the building functions as a museum rather than a synagogue.

above – including Ibn Zulaq, al-Musabbihi, and Ibn al-Tuwayr – are mainly known to us because al-Maqrizi cites them at length in his books. In his own writings, al-Maqrizi reveals an acute awareness of how misinformation about the Fatimids had become endemic. He sought to buck the trend, arguing for reliance on contemporary Egyptian sources in the reportage of events:

> Ibn Zulaq was better informed than Ibn al-Athir about events in Egypt, particularly those concerning al-Muʿizz, as he was present and witnessed them . . . Ibn al-Athir, on the other hand, has based his information on the Iraqi and Syrian historians. It is clear to those who have delved into the study of historical accounts that the latter are much prejudiced against the Fatimid caliphs and say abominable things about them, despite the fact that their knowledge of the conditions in Egypt is extremely limited.[2]

From the 10th to the 12th century, the works of Fatimid Ismaili scholars, including Qadi al-Nuʿman (d. 974), al-Sijistani (d. after 971), al-Nisaburi (d. after 996), al-Kirmani (d. 1021), and al-Shirazi (d. 1078), among others, became crucial repositories of law, literature, history, and philosophy for adherents of the Fatimid *daʿwa*. Their writings were disseminated to Ismaili communities living outside the Fatimid realms, and there found sanctuary upon the waning of the dynasty. Largely preserved in private libraries, such works began to publicly resurface in the 20th century. Notable among these is the multivolume *Uyun al-akhbar wa funun al-athar* written in the 15th century by Idris Imad al-Din (d. 1468), a Tayyibi Ismaili scholar from Yemen. In composing this work, Imad al-Din drew upon a range of earlier Fatimid sources, several of which are lost today.

The publication of rediscovered texts and the continued study of literary and documentary sources have advanced our knowledge of Fatimid history and historiography. The increasing avail-ability of alternative viewpoints, empathic or hostile, has been especially important in foster-ing balanced and critically aware readings on the Fatimids. Such critical approaches to the sources remain pivotal today as Fatimid studies continues to flourish.

The Spread of the Empire

While in Ifriqiya, the Imam-caliph al-Mu'izz had commissioned a map of the world. As we shall see in Chapter 6, the sciences of cartography had rapidly advanced in the Muslim world and were to find creative expression in Fatimid Egypt. The map commissioned by al-Mu'izz in time came to adorn a wall in the royal mausoleum of Cairo. It is described in the following extract:

A piece of fine blue silk, a magnificent artifact, with gold lettering and with various pieces of silk stitched on, a work of al-Mu'izz; on it were pictured the parts of the earth, with all the cities and mountains, seas and rivers, a reproduction of geography [*al-jughrafiyya*]; Mecca and Medina were portrayed on it, and below it [was written]: 'Completed at the command of al-Muʿizz li-Din Allah, out of longing for the Sanctuary of God, and in order to make known the places of the Messenger of God, in the year 353 (964).'[3]

The Fatimids' acquisition of Egypt reshaped the geography of their empire, which by 973 extended over vast terrains. To the west, Fatimid lands encompassed Ifriqiya and some of the Maghreb (including present-day Algeria and parts of Morocco). Prior to his departure, al-Muʿizz had entrusted Ifriqiya to Buluggin b. Ziri (d. 984), a Berber chieftain from the Sanhaja tribe whose forefathers had been loyal supporters of the Imam-caliphs. Buluggin's appointment signalled the beginning of the subsequent Zirid dynasty (972–1148), which ruled under the Fatimid banner until 1048/1049.

The Fatimid domain in the 970s also included the rich and fertile island of Sicily, which had come under Fatimid suzerainty soon after 909. Fatimid patronage of its capital city, Palermo, took its most enduring form with the building of the Khalisa quarters, known today as the 'Kalsa' district near the city centre. Fatimid Sicily reached its pinnacle under the Kalbid family, which ruled as Fatimid governors for the better part of a century and oversaw a sustained era of investment in trade and agriculture before being defeated by the Normans in 1061.

From Ifriqiya eastwards, Fatimid rule extended across the coastlands of Libya and Cyrenaica, encompassing the towns of Tripoli and Barqa. In Egypt itself, Fatimid sovereignty extended from the Mediterranean coast in the north, including Alexandria, down to Upper Egypt, including Aswan, in the south and towards the Red Sea coast. To the east, Fatimid reach extended into Palestine and Syria – a hold that remained tenuous, however, with events there dominating Fatimid foreign policy in the centuries that followed.

The most prestigious and symbolically import-ant lands over which the Fatimids held suzerainty were those of the *haramayn* (the two sanctuaries) of Mecca and Medina – the first the site of the Ka'ba and the Holy Mosque (*Masjid al-Haram*), the second of the Prophet's Mosque and his tomb. Earlier in the mid-10th century, Mecca and Medina had been in turmoil. While under nominal Abbasid rule, power over the two cities was held by two prominent clans of the *ashraf*, who by the 950s had come to violent clashes. When news of this reached al-Mu'izz, as their distant blood-relative, he sent mediators and underwrote the compensation owed to the injured parties. Two decades later, when the Fatimids entered Egypt, the *amir* of Mecca proclaimed al-Mu'izz the *amir al-mu'minin*. Soon, Medina followed suit. The proclamations of al-Mu'izz's legitimate rule displaced two centuries of Abbasid suzerainty over the *haramayn*, which would continue in the Fatimid name for much of the next century.

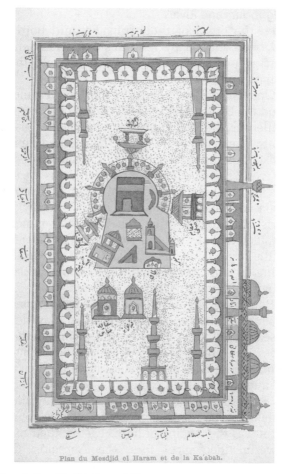

Figure 6. Map of the Holy Mosque in Mecca

Map of the Masjid al-Haram, Mecca. Page taken from the *Sefer Nameh. Relation du voyage de Nassiri Khosrau en Syrie, en Palestine, en Egypte, en Arabie et en Perse, pendant les Années de l'Hégire 437–444 (1035–1042)*, published, translated, and annotated by Charles Schefer (Paris, 1881).

Neighbours and Rivals

From the onset of their rule, Fatimid borders had been shaped by relationships with neighbouring powers, many of whom upheld their own claim to universal rule.

On the northern shores of the Mediterranean stood the Byzantine Empire. While facing its own challenges, the Byzantines had undergone a major resurgence in the 10th century. Their grand capital Constantinople (today's Istanbul) remained one of the world's great cities, and its position as the site of a patriarchate and home of the sixth-century Hagia Sophia symbolized the centrality of Christianity to Byzantine rule. With their emperor considered God's rightful ruler and the defender of the true faith, the Byzantines' universalist claims to authority echoed those of the Fatimids in Cairo and the Abbasids in Baghdad.

Bound by the waters of the Mediterranean, Fatimid and Byzantine rivalries often played out at sea, initially centring on Sicily and southern Italy, with Byzantine ambassadors becoming a recurring presence at the Fatimid court. When the Fatimid focus shifted eastwards, so did the locus of Fatimid–Byzantine rivalry. Soon, northern Syria would become their next major battleground. But it was the locking of horns against their most powerful ideological foes, the Abbasids, that continued to occupy Fatimid attention.

The Fatimid–Abbasid Rivalry

The arrival of the Fatimids in North Africa had seen the overthrow of the Aghlabids, and their

entry into Egypt had seen the overthrow of the
Ikhshidids. Both had ruled as Abbasid viceroys.
When news first arrived in Ifriqiya of Jawhar's
arrival in Egypt, the famous Fatimid-court poet
Ibn Hani al-Andalusi (d. 973) celebrated the
moment in verse:

> The Abbasids say, 'Has Egypt been
>   conquered?'
> Tell the Abbasids, 'The matter has been
>   ordained!'
> . . .
> So do not dwell upon the memory of an age
>   that has now passed away. That age is
>   now bygone; this [now] is a [new] age.[4]

Ibn Hani himself would not see Cairo, dying in
mysterious circumstances as he travelled with
al-Mu'izz's entourage to Egypt. But his verses
circulated widely and belied the deep rivalry
between the descendants of Ali and the Abbasid
house.

The bitter hostility of the Abbasids towards
Shi'i movements stemmed initially from the simil-
arity in their claims to authority. The Shi'i claim
that authority was vested in the descendants of Ali
and Fatima negated the Abbasid claim that authority was vested, rather, in their own family, the
descendants of the Prophet's uncle al-Abbas. The
first centuries of the Abbasid caliphate had seen
sustained persecutions of Shi'i movements and
the arrest and killing of Shi'i Imams. But the ascent
of the Shi'i Fatimids posed an unprecedented

challenge to the Abbasids. Unable to curb the Fatimid expansion or the flourishing of the Ismaili *da'wa*, the caliphs of Baghdad and their supporters turned instead towards sustained propaganda to counter the Fatimid advance.

By the 10th century, however, the Abbasid caliphs were subservient to their military overlords, the *amir*s of the Buyid confederation (945–1055). Though expressing Shiʿi affinities and appealing to Persian ideals of monarchy, the Buyid rulers had maintained the Abbasid caliphs as nominal sovereigns to legitimize their own rule over predominantly Sunni territories. When the Fatimids arrived in Egypt, the Buyids were at the height of their power under their leading *amir* Adud al-Dawla (d. 983). Adud's death would soon, however, precipitate Buyid decline and pave the path for a resurgence in the Abbasid caliph's authority.

The Contest for Syria

Syria – sitting in proximity to Fatimid Egypt, Byzantine Anatolia, and Abbasid Iraq – was to become the principal scene of rivalries between the region's major powers. The country was then suffering from its own fractious internal dynamics. Syria's northern regions, including Aleppo, were ruled by *amir*s of the Hamdanid dynasty (905–1004); they had Shiʿi proclivities but governed in the Abbasid name. In southern Syria, the Ikhshidids had controlled Damascus since 935; however, with their demise in 969 local militias gained power. Meanwhile, across the

Syrian desert, resurging Bedouin tribes had emerged once more as a powerful force.

It was the Qaramita, however, that initially proved most hostile and dangerous to the Fatimid advance in Syria after 969. The Qaramita arose out of the Ismaili *da'wa* of the late ninth century. During the 'period of concealment' when the *da'wa* first flourished, many in the *da'wa* had held that the eighth-century Ismaili Imam, Muhammad b. Ismail b. Ja'far, would return as the messianic *al-mahdi* (the rightly guided one). Belief in the emergence of the *mahdi* – the messiah who would restore justice to the world – was then widespread. But when the *da'wa* organization pronounced that the line of the Imams continued in the descendants of Muhammad b. Ismail – and the *mahdi* was now manifest in the person of the first Fatimid Imam-caliph Abd Allah al-Mahdi – a group of dissident *da'i*s broke away to chart their own course. Initially led by Hamdan Qarmat, from whom they gained their name, the Qaramita forged alliances with Bedouin tribes and by the early 10th century formed an independent powerbase in eastern Arabia. In time they would become infamous, especially for stealing the sanctified black stone (*al-hajar al-aswad*) from the Ka'ba and for regular pillaging of the *hajj* caravans. After 969, they became amongst the most bitter opponents of the Fatimids, not least because the Fatimid protection of the pilgrimage routes was robbing them of a crucial source of revenue. In August 971, it was a Qarmati assault that had defeated the Fatimid army in Damascus, which was followed by the Qaramita's march to Cairo. Jawhar's then resolute defence of the city had only, however, temporarily deferred their threat.

The Consolidation of Egypt and the Final Years of al-Mu'izz's reign

The settlement of al-Mu'izz in Cairo in June 973 saw the first manifestation of a living Shi'i imamate in Egypt: new expressions of faith and practice became hallmarks of public life. In the years that followed, the Imam-caliph oversaw efforts to buttress the Fatimid presence through a policy of reconciliation. To this end, he welcomed dignitaries from across Egypt to an audience at his palace and granted pardons to numerous opponents, including over a thousand Ikhshidid soldiers who had been captured during Jawhar's earlier campaigns.

Instability on the eastern borders continued to fester, however. By March 974, the Qaramita had marched once more upon Egypt. This time, the Fatimid army led by al-Mu'izz's son and heir apparent, the prince Abd Allah, achieved a decisive victory. Yet, less than a year after the celebrations of Abd Allah's triumph, the Fatimid household suffered grief as the prince himself passed away unexpectedly.

The Restoration of the Hajj *Caravans*

In July 975, a much-awaited official announcement was made at the great *Jami al-Atiq* (the Old Mosque) in Fustat, known as the Mosque of Amr

Figure 7. The Mosque of Amr b. al-As, Fustat
Partial view of the courtyard and ablutions fountain of the Mosque of Amr b.
al-As as it looks today after many episodes of reconstruction.

b. al-As today. It declared that the *hajj* caravan
would proceed on land. For years, pilgrimage
caravans leaving Egypt for Mecca had been
stymied by Qaramati and Bedouin assaults.
Following the announcement, and with the route
secured, Egypt's *hajj* pilgrims departed. Upon
their return in October, they reported that:

> The *daʿwa* was proclaimed [in al-Muʿizz's
> name] at Mecca . . . They also reported that
> the pilgrimage had been completed.
>   This was the first season in which
> al-Muʿizz's name was pronounced in the
> sermon in Mecca and in the city of the
> Prophet [Medina].[5]

Patronage and protection of the *hajj* was long considered a principal responsibility of any caliph and was among the guarantees stipulated in the Fatimid *aman*. Suzerainty of the holy lands also entailed providing protection from hunger, so the sending of grain and foodstuff from Egypt to the Hijaz was to remain a crucial feature of the relationship between Fatimid Egypt and the *haramayn*. Patronage also entailed responsibility for beautifying the sanctuary. Thus, the custom of sending the *kiswa* (the cloth covering) to the Ka'ba along with other adornments became a Fatimid prerogative. The chronicles relate the resplendence of one decoration, the *shamsa*, a bejewelled suspended crown that had long served as an insignia of Muslim caliphates:

> On the day of Arafa, al-Mu'izz displayed the *shamsa*, which he had prepared for the Ka'ba, in the *iwan* (audience hall) of the palace. Its width and length were twelve *shibr* (hand-spans). Its base was made of red brocade. On its circumference were twelve gold crescents. To each crescent was linked a gold sphere. In the heart of each sphere were fifty pearls, white as dove-eggs and studded with rubies red, yellow, and blue. Around it were written verses from [Surat] al-Hajj [Q. 22].[6]

Towards Economic Reform

Repairing the damage that political instability had wreaked on Egypt's economy and replenishing the outlay expended during the Fatimid advance necessitated major financial and agrarian initiatives. To oversee these projects, al-Muʿizz appointed an accomplished financial expert, Yaʿqub b. Yusuf b. Killis, whom we will encounter in Chapter 3 as the first Fatimid vizier. Assisted by Ifriqiyan bureaucrats, Yaʿqub b. Killis oversaw the recalculation of the taxable areas of the country, resulting in substantial increases to the treasury.

Another critical Fatimid reform was the restoration of coinage. Debasement of the currency by addition of impurities to the precious metals during minting had long plagued Egypt, resulting in unreliable pricing and inflation. Among the proclamations of the *aman*, perhaps most resonant for merchants was the promise that the Fatimids would 'renew the coinage'.[7] This saw the institution of Fatimid 'Muʿizzi' dinars as the state currency. While the substitutions of coinage initially led to major con-sternation regarding exchange rates, the Fatimid dinar eventually became the predominant medium of trade. Highly valued on international trading networks for their gold content, the Fatimid dinars provided a major impetus for the expansion of trade in the ensuing years.

Fatimid economic reforms also introduced policies to regulate market prices. A pernicious issue afflicting Egypt was the hoarding of essential food items by speculators aiming to drive up prices in times of perceived shortage. With the supply of produce ever subservient to the fluctuations of the Nile, knowledge of how much the river had risen

Figure 8. Coin of al-Mu'izz
The obverse (left) and reverse (right) of a gold coin minted in Egypt
in 969. The inner circle of the reverse of the coin carries the name of al-Mu'izz.
The outer circle of the obverse quotes Q. 9:33: 'Muhammad is the messenger
of God who sent him with guidance and the religion of truth . . .' (excerpted
here). The inscriptions in their entirety can be found on the website of the
David Collection.

directly impacted market prices. Al-Maqrizi
relates that, soon after arriving in Egypt, al-Mu'izz
regulated the custom of announcing the Nile's rise
so that 'only when it had reached its level of
sixteen cubits was the announcement to be made
public'.[8] In his *Khitat*, a substantive work on
Egypt's topography, al-Maqrizi writes approvingly
about the regulation:

> Reflect on what a wonderful policy this was.
> For the people used to always halt by the
> Nile during the days of its increase. If it rose
> a little, they would get agitated and would
> discuss among themselves the absence of the
> rising of the Nile. Then they would hoard
> the produce and would refuse to sell it, in
> the hope of a rise in prices. Those who had

wealth would stock up the produce, either to fetch high prices or to amass food for their family. Because of this, the prices increased dramatically.[9]

Al-Muʿizz's rule in Egypt lasted less than three years. In 975, aged 44, he passed away after a brief illness. While the world he left behind had irrevocably changed, the age of the Fatimids in Egypt had only just begun.

Chapter 3

Towards an Inclusive Empire

The People of Egypt

The patterns of life in Egypt were deeply etched in the memory of the indigenous Coptic community. Peasants had worked the land from time immemorial, bequeathing their agrarian wisdom across generations. With their expertise in local government also often passed down the generations, Coptic officials had long been indispensable in the governing of Egypt during both Byzantine and Muslim rule. The Copts were then the largest of Egypt's Christian communities. Others included the Melkite Christians, so called because of their adherence to the imperial (*malaki*) Christianity of the Byzantines. Also present in the country were the Nestorian Christians, a community that also had links with the Christians of Syria, Iraq, and other eastern regions.

With their history in the country stretching back to the biblical era, Jewish communities were also settled across Egypt. By the 10th century, they included the Qaraite and Rabbanite traditions, with the former upholding a more literalist understanding of the written Torah and the latter maintaining the authority of the Talmud. Jewish traders were especially important to the Egyptian economy, linking the thriving worlds of the Mediterranean and the Indian Ocean. Jewish physicians were similarly prominent, included amongst them Musa b. Azar, the personal physician of al-Muʿizz.

Egypt's Muslim populace also reflected the rich diversity of faiths in the country. Sunni Muslims belonging to the Maliki and Shafiʿi legal schools probably constituted the majority in Alexandria and Fustat, the latter city being the site of the tomb of the famed Sunni jurist and eponym of the Shafiʿi *madhhab*, Muhammad b. Idris al-Shafiʿi (d. 820). Shiʿi Muslims were also long-established in the country, including adherents of the Ismaili *daʿwa* who had been instrumental in facilitating the Fatimid entry.

Among the diverse communities were also an array of ethnicities, enrichened by new waves of migration in recent decades. The weakening of the Abbasid caliphate had shifted the trade routes towards the Red Sea, leading many Iraqi and Iranian merchants and artisans to migrate westwards and settle in Egypt, as did large groups of Turkish soldiers. With the arrival of the Fatimids, thousands of Kutama Berbers – called the westerners (*al-maghariba*) in the chronicles – made Egypt their home, as did in time Nubians, Sudanese, and Armenians. While the diverse peoples enriched Egyptian life, religious and ethnic rivalries would remain a perennial challenge to Fatimid governance.

Figure 9. Map (Cropped) Showing the Tomb of al-Shafiʿi
Illustration of the city of Cairo showing the Tomb of al-Shafiʿi, taken from a folio
of the 'Book on Navigation' by the Ottoman navigator and cartographer Piri
Reis (d. 1555), late 17th to early 18th century.

The Dhimma of the Imam

When the *aman* was publicly read out in 969,
central to the proclamation and salient to the
varied religious confessions was the pronouncement of the Fatimid Imam's *dhimma* (guarantee):

I guarantee you God's complete and universal safety . . . for your lives, your property, your families, your livestock, your estates and your quarters, and whatever you possess, be it modest or significant.[1]

The doctrine of the *dhimma* served as a bedrock of Fatimid governance. Anchored in the Imam-caliph's claim to universal authority, the *dhimma* declared that all the subjects of the empire, regardless of religion or ethnicity, came under the protective canopy of the Fatimid sovereign. This notion hearkened back to a pivotal Qur'anic principle and to the precedent set by the Prophet Muhammad when he extended God's guarantee of safety and protection to the people of Medina, an idea encapsulated in the famous document generally known today as 'the Constitution of Medina'. This notion of the protective canopy of the *dhimma* came, in time, to encompass Christians and Jews living under the earlier Muslim caliphates. As people of the scriptures (*ahl al-kitab*), they were seen as legitimate recipients of the mantle of God's protection, thus becoming the *ahl al-dhimma* (people of the guarantee). The Fatimid Imam-caliphs – doctrinally proclaimed as inheritors of the Prophet's authority – considered the provision of their own *dhimma* to be an extension of God's guarantee, a prerogative assumed by each successive Imam.

The Succession of Nizar al-Aziz bi'llah (975–996)
In December 975, the crowds that were gathered for the Friday sermon at Fustat's Old Mosque

heard a special pronouncement by the prayer
leader in his benedictions:

> O God, support him [al-Muʿizz] and strengthen
> his triumph through Prince Nizar Abu'l-
> Mansur, the heir apparent [*wali al-ahd*] of
> the Muslims, the son of the Commander of the
> Faithful, whom You have made *al-qaʾim* (the
> executor) of his *daʿwa* and of his proof.[2]

Born in al-Mahdiyya in 955, Prince Nizar was
the third son of al-Muʿizz, and was aged 16 when
he accompanied his father to Egypt. Nizar's physical features and character must have been striking,
for the contemporary historian al-Musabbihi took
the time to describe them:

> He had reddish hair, his eyes were large
> and dark blue, his shoulders broad. Kind
> in disposition and close to the people, he
> disliked shedding blood.[3]

For the later Egyptian biographer Ibn Khallikan
(d. 1282), however, it was Nizar's personal traits
that were most noteworthy: 'The new sovereign
was generous, brave and inclined to forgiveness,
even with the power of punishing.'[4]

When the Qaramita marched into Egypt in
974, Nizar was probably among those who set
out to repel them under the command of his
elder brother, Abd Allah b. al-Muʿizz. When Abd
Allah passed away, however, after a short but
acute illness in February 975, the question of
succession came to the fore. By the end of the

year, and prior to al-Mu'izz's demise, the announcement of Nizar as heir apparent was proclaimed. In Fatimid sources, the transfer of the succession from al-Mu'izz to Nizar was presented as foreordained. As later relayed by al-Maqrizi, it was recorded in a conversation transmitted from Nizar himself, where on an occasion when Nizar was walking alongside his brothers Abd Allah and Tamim, al-Mu'izz had told his younger son Nizar, 'It [the imamate] is coming to you.'[5]

Nizar was aged 20 when his father passed away in December 975, and he took the regnal title *al-Aziz bi'llah* (the Glorious by God). No sooner had his reign begun, however, than strife in Syria erupted once again.

The Struggle for Syria and the Inclusion of the Turks

The turmoil of earlier decades had continued to fester in Syria. Especially pressing was the seemingly relentless Byzantine advance. Since the mid-10th century, esteemed Byzantine generals had re-established their empire's rule over numerous border regions in Syria, including the city of Antioch. The loss of Muslim cities had been strongly felt and galvanizing the struggle against the Byzantines was among the signal features of the Fatimid *aman*.

Alp Tegin and the Turkish Contingents

In 976, a new commander raised his banner over Damascus. Alp Tegin was a veteran Turkish

general who had once served the Buyids before
being exiled. When excesses and pillaging by
Fatimid Kutama soldiers stoked resentment in
Damascus, local leaders forged an alliance
with Alp Tegin to expel the Fatimid governor.
Having seized Damascus, Alp Tegin launched a
ferocious assault on Fatimid armies elsewhere
in Syria and Palestine. Within a year, Fatimid
garrisons at Sidon and Tiberias were defeated,
and Fatimid chiefs and *da'i*s were put to the
sword.

Al-Aziz bi'llah turned to the veteran
commander Jawhar, now in his late fifties, to lead
an army of 20,000 Kutama Berbers to confront Alp
Tegin. The expedition proved disastrous, being
beset by snow and dwindling supplies. After
besieging Damascus, Jawhar's army was forced to
retreat to the Mediterranean coast in the face of a
new military alliance between Alp Tegin and the
Qaramita. There, Jawhar had to negotiate humili-
ating terms of surrender.

With the situation now critical, al-Aziz
resolved to take to the battlefield in person,
leading a new Fatimid expedition eastward in
978. At the border regions of Egypt and Palestine,
bolstered by new allies from the Arab Jarrahid
tribe, the Fatimid armies met those of Alp Tegin's
confederation in battle. The Fatimid sovereign
secured a significant victory, and soon Alp Tegin
was seized by the Bedouin allies of the Fatimids
and brought shackled to al-Aziz's encampment.
Though many may have expected his execution,
al-Aziz decided otherwise. The contemporary

Christian historian Yahya al-Antaki relates the clemency al-Aziz extended to Alp Tegin:

> Al-Aziz rescued Alp Tegin from his captors, the Turk being close to death. He then granted Alp Tegin an *aman* personally, handing over his signet ring to him. The Turk asked for water, and al-Aziz ordered a goblet of iced rose water to be brought. The Turk hesitated from drinking it, fearing that it may be poisoned. Al-Aziz realised this, and so he took the goblet and drank from it. The Turk drank the rest.[6]

For Fatimid court notables, what followed was perhaps unexpected. On the Fatimid army's triumphant return march, al-Aziz gave Alp Tegin pride of place, with the Turkish general's companions freed and allowed to ride by his side. Upon their arrival in Cairo, al-Aziz ordered that Alp Tegin and his people were to be treated with respect and courtesy. For some, the clemency proved challenging. A leading Egyptian *sharif*, Ibrahim al-Rassi, wrote to al-Aziz in complaint. The Imam-caliph responded in person saying that having once promised kindness to Alp Tegin, and with God having granted him victory, 'Is it becoming of me not to fulfil my promise?'[7]

Sharper-eyed courtiers may well have discerned portents of impending change. The Fatimid military experience in Syria demonstrated that their army required an overhaul. For over 80 years, Kutama tribesmen with their solid formations of foot soldiers had stood as the vanguard of the military. Yet the Syrian terrain demanded a different strategy. Here, the model perfected by the Turkish contingents, of charging waves of mounted archers and cavalrymen, proved far superior.

Thereafter, al-Aziz initiated a series of military reforms, reflecting similar developments in the Muslim east. He integrated Alp Tegin into the Fatimid military, and this mobilized the enlisting of new contingents of Turks. Large numbers of Turkish slave-soldiers of Central Asian origin soon occupied a quarter in the Fatimid capital. Thereafter, their battalions fought under Fatimid banners, producing new generations of noted generals and loyal supporters of the Fatimid realms. While al-Aziz's reforms rejuvenated the Fatimid army, they also altered its ethnic makeup; rivalries between the old guard and the recent recruits soon ensued.

The New Administration of Egypt

When Jawhar first entered Egypt, he had been accompanied by several officials from the Fatimid state in North Africa who may have been expected to replace the bureaucrats of the previous Ikhshidid government. However, al-Mu'izz had stipulated that many of the Egyptian officials were to be retained, including the famous Sunni chief judge, the *qadi* Abu Tahir. The North-African officials were initially appointed alongside Egypt's bureaucrats to work in joint roles. This sharing of offices minimized the disruptions wrought by the transfer of government and became one of many steps taken by the Fatimids in developing an inclusive system of governance, one exemplified by the rise of Ya'qub b. Killis.

The First Fatimid Vizier and the Ahl al-Kitab in the Fatimid Administration

Ya'qub b. Yusuf b. Killis, commonly known as Ibn Killis, was born in 930 to a Jewish family living in Baghdad. In his teens he made his way to Syria where he gained employment as an agent for local merchants before later moving to Fustat. There, Ibn Killis gained the trust of Egypt's then ruler Kafur al-Ikhshidi and rose in the administration, until Kafur decreed to his officials that 'not a dinar [nor a dirham] should be paid without Ya'qub's authorization'.[8] In 967, aged 37, Ibn Killis became a Muslim. Taking to his new faith with earnestness, he hired a scholar well versed in the Qur'an and spent his nights reading scripture. When Kafur died a year later, however, Ibn Killis's fortunes turned as rivals, perhaps resentful of his meteoric rise, had him arrested. After securing his freedom, he set out towards Ifriqiya, meeting up with the Fatimid army advancing to Egypt. Thereafter, Ibn Killis entered the service of al-Mu'izz. In 973, he was entrusted with overseeing much of Egypt's administration, including the fiscal reforms:

> Sixteen days before the end of Muharram [14 October 973], al-Mu'izz appointed the

vizier Abu'l-Faraj Ya'qub b. Yusuf [b. Killis]
and Usluj b. al-Hasan to oversee the land-tax
and all other taxes, the supervision of markets,
the river coast, the poll-tax, religious endowments, inheritance, the two *shurta*s [police
forces], and all other related responsibilities
over Fustat and all the provinces.[9]

The Fatimid treasury flourished. It was during
al-Aziz's reign that Ibn Killis's career reached its
apogee – in April 979, he was appointed the
first Fatimid vizier (*wazir*, meaning helper). The
institution of the vizierate (*wizara*) had by then
existed in the Muslim world for almost two
centuries, with the office corresponding to that
of a chief minister of state. On behalf of the
Imam-caliph, the vizier Ibn Killis oversaw the
armed forces, the markets and the treasury,
finance and taxation, intelligence and commu-
nication, matters relating to the *hajj* pilgrimage,
and the adjudication of grievances against state
officials.

Ibn Killis served as vizier for almost 12 years.
In time, he would be ranked among the most
influential viziers of medieval Muslim history.
Nonetheless, his status was not inviolable.
When accused of poisoning Alp Tegin, whom
Ibn Killis had regarded as a rival, the vizier was
removed from office by al-Aziz. Once reinstated,
however, Ibn Killis continued in the position
until his demise in 991.

The vizierate became a pivotal position in
the Fatimid administration, and while Ya'qub

served as a Muslim official and would himself compose a work on Ismaili law, his ascent coincided with the rise of both Christians and Jews through the ranks of Fatimid government.

The prominence of Jews and Christians in the Fatimid government has elicited much interest among modern historians. The involvement of Christian officials in Muslim Egypt was not unprecedented, with Coptic administrators having held important roles in previous dynasties. The public role of Jews and Christians in the Fatimid period was, however, seemingly distinct. Historians once reasoned that this was a consequence of the Fatimids being an Ismaili Shi'i minority that relied on non-Muslim groups to administer their lands. More recently, however, some historians have noted this as a natural consequence of the Fatimid Imam's universal extension of the *dhimma*, whereby all those under his obedience were afforded the opportunity to hold public office.

In 996, al-Aziz appointed Isa b. Nestorius as chief minister, the first time a Christian official had been appointed to this pre-eminent role. Little is known about Isa's early life, but it is probable that like other Christians of his background, Isa first built his reputation in the *diwan al-kharaj* (the department of taxation). During this period, the Jews of the Fatimid Empire also witnessed the rise of their co-religionists, exemplified in the figure of Menashshe b. al-Qazzaz. Menashshe was the son of a silk merchant and had a distinguished career in Syria and had become Ya'qub

b. Killis's leading agent in the region. Following Ya'qub's passing, al-Aziz appointed Menashshe as the *katib al-jaysh* (head administrator of the army). Thereafter, he was promoted to the post of Fatimid governor of Syria.

Managing Diverse Communities

Pope Abraham of Alexandria (d. 978) was the 62nd patriarch of the Coptic Church. Early in al-Aziz's reign, he came to the Imam-caliph's court with a particular request.

The old Coptic church of St Mercurius near Fustat had fallen into ruin. Used for a while to store sugarcane, little now remained of it except the outer walls. In his visit, Pope Abraham sought al-Aziz's authorization to rebuild the holy site. The Imam-caliph granted permission and offered funds for its restoration. But when news of this spread across the city, a group of Muslim agitators arrived at the site and hindered its reconstruction. Soldiers were dispatched to disperse them and allow the work to progress.

Managing the expectations of Egypt's diverse communities remained an intractable challenge in the country's governance. Under the Fatimids, each of the religious communities were afforded specified rights and duties, but in the public sphere Fatimid rule of law prevailed. Elements from the Muslim populace nonetheless were angered, especially at the promotion of Christians and Jews through government ranks. Some medieval Muslim sources record that when al-Aziz was riding through Cairo, he came across a paper effigy in whose hand a note had been attached:

> By the One who made the Jews mighty through Menashshe, and the Christians through Isa b. Nestorius, and humiliated the Muslims through you, will you not investigate my case?[10]

The protestations against Isa and Menashshe were seemingly not entirely unwarranted. Just as Muslim agitators baited for privilege, other reports suggest that several Christian and Jewish officials in government promoted their own co-religionists at the expense of Muslim officials. Accordingly, al-Aziz had the two officials apprehended, but they were released in due course. Their arrest probably served as a warning to others promoting privileges based on religious affiliation. The reigns of al-Mu'izz and al-Aziz are nonetheless cited in the sources for the protection and opportunity they presented to Egypt's diverse communities. For the medieval authors of the famous *History of the Patriarchs of the Coptic Church of Alexandria*, this was an era when 'there was great peace for the churches'.[11]

Al-Aziz and Christian Familial Relations

Al-Aziz's affiliation with the Christian community extended into his own household. While in Ifriqiya, he had taken as consort a lady who probably stemmed from a family of Melkite Christian patriarchs. Known simply as *al-Sayyida al-Aziziyya* (al-Aziz's Lady), she remained his lifelong companion. While the Sayyida would become one of the most influential and affluent women of her age, little is known about her biography. She was apparently born in Sicily and probably raised in a Greek-speaking household. Her father seems to have been a Melkite monk to whom al-Aziz granted control of a fortress in Sicily and perhaps even a monastery to which he could retire. Al-Aziz and al-Sayyida had a daughter who was given the title *Sitt al-Mulk* (Lady of the Empire). Sitt al-Mulk was presented by the chronicles as the apple of her father's eye, but even so, few could have then imagined the pivotal role she would play in the decades that followed.

Through these familial relations, al-Aziz developed a close relationship with the Melkite Christians. Two of al-Sayyida's brothers, Arsenius and Orestes, were educated in the doctrines of the Melkite confession, and, in 986, both were appointed to the highest ranks of the Melkite Church. In Fatimid Jerusalem, a city with a significant Melkite presence, Orestes was appointed patriarch, an office he retained for two decades. Thereafter, he was part of a Fatimid delegation to Constantinople. Similarly, Arsenius was appointed the metropolitan of the Melkite communities in Cairo and Fustat, before later becoming the grand patriarch of Alexandria. Sitt al-Mulk maintained close relations with her maternal uncles. Upon his demise, Arsenius is said to have left a precious collection of vestments, chalices, and other valuable gifts for his niece, who later donated them to a church in Alexandria.

The close bond between al-Aziz, al-Sayyida, and Sitt al-Mulk becomes especially evident in accounts concerning al-Sayyida's demise in November 995, when al-Aziz was at a military encampment outside Cairo. Both father and daughter escorted her bier back to the capital, and having recited the funerary prayer over her, al-Aziz himself placed her in the royal tomb. Sitt al-Mulk, then 24 years old, remained by her graveside for a month. Though he had to return to the encampment, al-Aziz rode back to Cairo to visit his grieving daughter almost daily and donated much in charity for the salvation of his departed companion.

Chapter 4

The Composition of the State

Within decades of its foundation, Cairo was well on its way to becoming a thriving metropolis. The maturing of the empire and its capital was underpinned by the development of complex government institutions and a legal system which regulated relations between state and society. Among the quintessential features of the new state was the public celebration of festivals and ceremonies that sought to symbolically convey the unity of the empire's peoples under the canopy of the universal imamate, one that would be increasingly tested as new challenges appeared on the horizon.

Cairo: A New Metropolis

Cairo was first laid out as a square city, approximately a kilometre in both directions, surrounded by towering mud-brick walls. Beyond its western edge was the famous Nile canal (*khalij*), an artificial waterway that cut away from the river and extended to the Red Sea. A short way beyond the western walls lay the Nile and the bustling port of al-Maqs. To the east were the Muqattam cliffs, a high rocky escarpment. The city's northern walls faced the lands

that extended into the Nile delta; from the southern walls, roads led to several urban settlements,
and then onto Fustat. Monumental gates marked
the city's entry points, and their names symbolically connected Cairo to the previous Fatimid
capitals: *Bab al-Futuh* (Gate of Conquests), *Bab
al-Fath* (Gate of Victory), and *Bab al-Zuwayla*
(Gate of Zuwayla). Several other gates would be
added over time to link the city to its burgeoning
suburbs.

The city was broadly divided by what became
known as the Great Road (*al-Shari al-A'zam*)
that intersected the city from north to south.
District names reflected the diverse makeup
of the capital: the Kutama quarter, the Turkish
quarter, the Roman quarter (where people of
Greek and Byzantine origins settled), and the
Daylami quarter (for the recent arrivals from
northern Iran). Elsewhere, districts were named
after key figures: the *Waziriyya* quarter housed
those once in the service of the vizier Ya'qub b.
Killis, while the *Jawdhariyya* district was home
to bureaucrats once linked to the esteemed
Fatimid administrator al-Ustadh Jawdhar.

Cairo first began as an exclusive royal city
reserved for the Imam-caliph's household and
those of the government and army, but markets,
bathhouses, and other amenities of everyday life
soon made their appearance as the city took
on an increasingly cosmopolitan character. In
time, and at its height, an estimated 120,000 to
200,000 people lived in the Fatimid capital. A
description of the city at its height was soon

to be penned by the famed *da'i* and poet Nasir-i
Khusraw:

> I estimated that there were no less than
> twenty thousand shops in Cairo ... There
> is no end of caravanserais, bathhouses and
> other public buildings ... The city of Cairo
> has five gates ... The buildings are even
> stronger and higher than the ramparts ...
> Most of the buildings are five storeys high,
> although some are six ... All the houses of
> Cairo are built separate from one another, so
> that no one's trees or outbuildings are against
> anyone else's walls.[1]

The Palace Complex and al-Azhar

At the heart of Cairo lay the Eastern Palace, home
to the Imam-caliphs and their households, and
often the location of the government offices. By
the 11th century, the Eastern Palace was a large
complex consisting of several buildings linked
through gardens and courtyards. It was contained
within a large outer wall of fine-cut stone. Each
building within the complex was named a palace
(*qasr*), and the sources name several: the Golden
Palace, the Women's Palace, the Prince's Palace,
the Victory Palace, the Tree Palace, and the
Breeze Palace. Dotted between them were storehouses, gardens, pavilions, kitchens, belvederes,
and other buildings.

Opposite the Eastern Palace, the Imam-caliph
al-Aziz had built the Western Palace, which he
eventually assigned to his daughter Sitt al-Mulk,

Figure 10. The Bayn al-Qasrayn

A reconstruction by Nezar al-Sayyad of the Bayn al-Qasrayn, the main thoroughfare of Fatimid Cairo, showing the Eastern and Western Palaces and the grand square between them.

and which came to include a great audience hall (*iwan*). The grand square (*maydan*) that opened up between the two places became known as the *Bayn al-Qasrayn* (Between the Palaces), the name invoking memories of a similar space at al-Mansuriyya and al-Mahdiyya.

To the south-east was Cairo's grand mosque, built by Jawhar soon after his arrival in 969. Called *al-Azhar* (the Radiant), it reflected one of the epithets of Fatima – *al-Zahra* – daughter of the Prophet Muhammad and foremother of the Fatimid Imam-caliphs. The mosque was built in just under nine months in broad rectangular form

Figure 11.   Courtyard of al-Azhar
A hand-coloured engraving by French lithographer Augustin François Lemaitre (d. 1870) of the Fatimid courtyard of al-Azhar, showing in the centre the 'royal' porch leading into the mosque. From *Égypte: Depuis la conquête des Arabes jusque à la domination française* (Paris, 1848).

and was aligned towards Mecca. Encompassed within its outer walls was a large open courtyard. This led towards a roofed indoor prayer hall in which Qur'anic inscriptions were elaborately carved in plaster. To this day, the al-Azhar Mosque remains an illustrious centre of learning in the Muslim world, and parts of its current structure are amongst the oldest surviving edifices of the Fatimid era.

The Government *Diwans*

Cairo's palace complex served multiple functions of statecraft, including receiving local dignitaries and foreign ambassadors. The operations of the state administration took place, however, in the *diwan*s. The term '*diwan*' (register, or office) refers to what would now correspond to an official 'department' of government. While *diwan*s were integral features of Muslim government from the seventh century onwards, the complex administrative system developed in Fatimid Egypt became one of the caliphate's lasting legacies. The number and functions of Fatimid *diwan*s evolved considerably over time, with the names, locations, and specific responsibilities of different *diwan*s changing during the reigns of different Imam-caliphs, or as per the reforms of different viziers and ministers. Many of their principal functions had, however, taken shape by al-Aziz's reign.

Pivotal was the department responsible for finance and taxation (*diwan al-kharaj*), which oversaw the collection of land taxes and revenues. Also crucial was the department of the army (*diwan al-jaysh*), which dealt with the recruitment and inspection of troops, and the maintenance of equipment. The *diwan al-ama'ir* (the department of construction) oversaw the Fatimid navy and was tasked with ensuring supplies of wood for new ships. The *diwan al-barid* (the postal service) was responsible for delivering correspondence using the road network, the navy or, commonly, carrier pigeons; it also fulfilled the vital function of gathering intelligence.

At various times, the *diwan al-majlis* (the office of audiences) stood particularly prominently, responsible for all the major affairs of state, including supervising public festivals. As the administration became increasingly complex, checks and balances became critical. Departments like the *diwan al-tahqiq* (the office of investigation) were created to oversee the conduct and expenditure of other *diwans*. Meticulous record-keeping practices that saw documents in one *diwan* duplicated in another also served the same function, and arrests and dismissals of officials often arose because of irregularities in correlated accounts.

Perhaps the most famous was the *diwan al-insha* (the office for correspondence), responsible for the official communications of the Imam-caliphs within the empire and with neighbouring powers. Such communications were often issued as official decrees known as *sijills* (from the Latin *sigillum*, meaning seal). These could range from specific administrative decrees to wide-ranging declarations that impacted Fatimid subjects at large and were often read out in public settings. *Sijill*s issued by the Imam-caliphs provide an important repository of official literature, often reflecting major milestones in the history of the Fatimid *da'wa* and *dawla*.

The treasury (*bayt al-mal*) was located in the Eastern Palace. It served as the main repository of state wealth and had specific storehouses (*khaza'in*) for high-value items. Trust in those supervising the *bayt al-mal* was paramount, and for decades the Imam-caliphs vested this responsibility in Muhammad b. al-Husayn b. al-Muhadhdhab (d. ca. early 11th century), a Fatimid Ifriqiyan official.

With the *diwan*s requiring extensive staffing, *kuttab* (scribes) of Muslim, Christian, and Jewish backgrounds formed the backbone of government. With a common grammar of statecraft and administration then prevailing across the Muslim world, the *kuttab* often travelled across different regions to further their careers, and many now saw new opportunities for advancement in Cairo. Qualifications and experience were vital. For the *diwan al-insha*, these included knowledge of formal diplomatic customs, eloquence, mastery of the Arabic language, and even an expert calligraphic hand. Careers in the *diwan*s also often followed lines of familial or social patronage, and *kuttab* of similar backgrounds gravitated towards the same specializations: those of Coptic backgrounds gravitated towards the *diwan* *al-kharaj*, whilst those of Arab Muslim backgrounds gravitated towards the *diwan*s of the army and the chancery.

The Pillars of Law and Justice

In April 988, news of a chilling crime rocked Fustat. A foreign merchant had been murdered in his residence, and all his possessions had been stolen. Word spread that one of Fustat's police officials was himself responsible, and public outrage heightened when it transpired that the same official had arrested innocent children of other merchants to pin the crime on. An anonymized letter soon reached al-Aziz to inform him about the events.

The case was recorded over a century later by Ibn al-Sayrafi (d. 1147), a famous 12th-century Fatimid *katib* and author, who headed the *diwan al-insha*, and whom we will encounter again in Chapter 8. Ibn al-Sayrafi reports that upon receiving the letter, al-Aziz ordered an immediate investigation by writing a note to Ibn Killis, excerpts of which follow:

> The letter [about the crime] reached us yesterday . . . How can this be under our protection and in our own lands? Let the vizier investigate this report thoroughly, so that he can seek retribution for God and for us, and so he can cleanse this disgrace from the *dawla* . . . It is incumbent upon you to report at length on the issue and to imprison the perpetrators until they disclose the truth.[2]

While Ibn al-Sayrafi does not mention what happened next, he notes that by his own time, the letter of al-Aziz was upheld as an exemplary model:

> All the Egyptians made copies of this decree. The pupils in schools were taught it . . .[3]

For medieval Muslims, the upholding of justice was central to notions of government, and they considered it a foremost responsibility of all rulers. This centrality was encapsulated in prophetic traditions that expressed preference for living under non-Muslim rulers who were just, rather than Muslim rulers who were unjust. With Egypt ravaged by lawlessness prior to the Fatimid arrival, the *aman*'s promise to uphold law and justice may well have struck a chord:

> The Commander of the Faithful . . . has advised his servant to extend equity and justice and to dispel injustice, to temper aggression, to eradicate transgression, to increase aid, to uphold what is just and to strengthen the oppressed through compassion and beneficence.[4]

Since its onset, the Fatimid legal system followed the general precepts of Shi'i Islamic law, with the Qur'an, the *sunna* of the Prophet Muhammad, and the *ta'lim* (authoritative teachings) of the Ismaili Imams serving as foundational precepts. During al-Mu'izz's reign, the system was formally codified by the pre-eminent Ismaili scholar of the age, Qadi Abu Hanifa al-Nuʿman. This culminated in al-Nuʿman's composition of the major legal compendium titled the *Daʿaʾim al-Islam* ('Pillars of Islam'), a work that became the primary reference for Fatimid jurists. In composing the work, al-Nuʿman relied on the guiding principles and authority of al-Muʿizz, who had instructed al-Nuʿman:

> [Draw] in your rulings and judgements on the Book of God ... Whenever you do not find the ruling regarding something in God's Book or in the Practice of the forefather of the Commander of the Faithful, Muhammad the Messenger of God ... seek it among the opinions of the Imams from his pure progeny, the devout and rightly guided ones, the fore-fathers of the Commander of the Faithful ... Whenever something continues to perplex you ... refer it ... to the Commander of the Faithful.[5]

In the Fatimid legal system, Ismaili law prevailed in the public sphere by regulating marketplaces, taxation, and the public calendar. Yet, following al-Mansur bi'llah's precedent, the Fatimid legal code recognized other Muslim legal schools, including the Sunni traditions. Where Fatimid law had not provided direct stipulation on legal matters – especially in those concerning personal law, such as divorce, inheritance, financial transactions, and distribution of assets between parties – the state authorized judges from the major Sunni *madhhab*s to hold court so that Sunni subjects could largely live by their own legal school, as also vouchsafed by the *aman*. This approach became evident early in Fatimid Egypt, with the appointment of two chief judges – an Ismaili Shiʻi and a Maliki Sunni – to head the judiciary:

> Abu'l-Hasan Ali [b. al-Qadi al-Nuʻman] was appointed by al-Muʻizz to act as the associate of Abu Tahir Muhammad in the post of *qadi* and chief magistrate . . . The two continued to act with joint authority till the death of al-Muʻizz and the accession of al-Aziz Nizar.[6]

Qadi al-Nuʻman had passed away in 974, soon after his arrival in Egypt. His eldest sons, Ali and Muhammad, continued his legacy, emerging as leading figures of Egypt's judiciary. In September 976, al-Aziz appointed Ali b. al-Nuʻman as chief judge, a role that included serving as lead Imam of the prayers, inspector of gold and silver coinage, and controller of weights and measures. As was customary for a chief judge, he was also appointed head of the *daʻwa*. When Ali passed away eight years later, his younger brother Muhammad stepped into the role. The legal codifications ushered in by al-Muʻizz and al-Nuʻman remained the bedrock of Fatimid law over the next centuries of the empire's rule.

The Public Ceremonials

On an Eid morning in 990, the people of Cairo awoke anticipating a day of momentous festivity. Many would have headed towards the gates of the Eastern Palace. There, a grand procession would have unfolded: African elephants steered by their riders, and a parade of exquisitely adorned horses ridden by horsemen clad in brocade embroidered with colourful patterns and floral reliefs, their swords glinting in the sunlight. All eyes would have then turned towards the *mizalla*, a white parasol, held high to signify that the Imam-caliph al-Aziz was riding beneath it. On his head was a bejewelled turban, and in his right hand, a staff (*qadib*) believed to be that of the Prophet. Behind him followed rows of senior officials and members of his own family.

In an air of sacrality and grandeur, the Imam-caliph's procession headed towards the northern gate. Along the route, state dignitaries were seated on benches (*mastaba*s) by the roadside. Passing through the northern wall, al-Aziz's procession then headed towards the *musalla* outside Cairo, an open space dedicated for festival prayers. There, the Imam-caliph ascended the *minbar*, a pulpit at the front of the prayer square. Salutations praising God filled the air. To commence the Eid prayers, the people in the *musalla* recited the *takbir*, proclaiming '*Allahu Akbar*' (God is Great). As their calls echoed, those seated on the *mastaba*s on the processional route also pronounced the *takbir*. From the *musalla* to the benches to the gates of the Eastern Palace, the *takbir*s formed a chain that reverberated through the city, ritually linking the *musalla* to the palace of the Imam.

Fatimid Egypt would become especially famous for its ritual processions and public festivals. While Eid processions marked Muslim holy days, numerous festivals of other religions were publicly celebrated across the calendar year. The Coptic calendar was replete with holy festivals, including those of the Coptic New Year, the Nativity, the Epiphany, and Maundy Thursday. Medieval accounts recount how Muslims joined some of these celebrations, as occasionally did the Imam-caliphs themselves. Public celebrations were also held to mark agrarian festivals that were germane to Egyptian life. Particularly important, and often attended by the Imam-caliphs, were annual ceremonies to 'break' open the dam at the entrance of the main canal (*kasr al-khalij*); these were held to mark the inundation of the Nile, a vital milestone in Egypt's agricultural calendar.

The holding of public processions served numerous functions for both state and society. As public performances, they symbolized the collective of those living under the Imam's *dhimma* and ritually linked the different urban regions to the palace of the Imam. Celebrations also, importantly, presented an opportunity for state largesse, through the sharing of communal meals and distribution of charity. Festivals and processions also served as a vital avenue for

direct contact between the sovereigns and the
populace; the latter could hand petitions to
the Imam-caliphs and seek redress to their
complaints. Centuries later, al-Maqrizi described
these occasions as 'the days that the Fatimid
caliphs observed as feasts and festivals through
which circumstances of the subjects were ameli-
orated, and their good fortune increased'.[7]

Durzan and the Qarafa Mosque

Fustat, which lay a few kilometres south of Cairo,
had been Egypt's capital for almost three centuries. In the Fatimid era it remained a large and
populous city, spanning 4 kilometres. At the
city's centre was the monumental Old Mosque
(*Jami al-Atiq*). Built soon after Fustat's foundation, it symbolized the city's role as a major centre
of Sunni scholarship. Imam-caliph al-Aziz visited
the mosque in person to break the Ramadan fast,
and he ordered the building of fountains that
served to beautify its interior.

South of Cairo and east of Fustat lay an area
called the Qarafa. A tranquil haven known for
its clement weather and clean water, the Qarafa
was also home to cemeteries and sacred spaces,
including tombs of the descendants of the *ahl
al-bayt*. It was in this ascetic setting that Durzan,
the consort of al-Mu'izz, had made her mark.

As the bulk of surviving chronicles were
written by male scholars of the medieval period,
women's experiences and contributions to the
era are mostly lost and rarely reported. It is
mainly through the painstaking reconstruction

of recent historians that women's involvement finds expression today.

Little is known about Durzan's background. Some sources claim that she was a cousin of al-Mu'izz, but most refer to her as an Arab slave who had a lilting voice, gaining her the nickname *Taghrid* (Tweeting Bird). At the Fatimid court she was referred to as *al-Sayyida al-Mu'izziya* (the Lady of al-Mu'izz). Durzan was the mother of al-Aziz, and she also bore a daughter who is only known by her title, *Sitt al-Malik* (Lady of the King).

In 976, Durzan ordered the building of a congregational mosque complex in the Qarafa. This was the first Fatimid mosque to be built in Egypt outside Cairo. Its location made it a focal point for residents of both Cairo and Fustat. Al-Maqrizi relates that on hot summer days, dignitaries from the Fatimid court would come to the Qarafa mosque to spend the night in its court-yard, while in winter they would sleep beside the pulpit of the mosque. Visitors marvelled at its eye-catching features. Not long after its construction, the famed geographer Ibn Hawqal (d. after 978) observed:

> It is one of the mosques distinguished by the spaciousness of its court, elegance of construction, and the fineness of its ceilings. In al-Jazira and Giza there are also *jami* (congregational) mosques, but they are inferior to the Qarafa mosque in splendor (*nabl*) and elegance (*husn*).[8]

The geographer al-Muqaddasi (d. 991) also visited the Qarafa and wrote about the 'handsomeness' of the mosque.[9] Others, too, recorded its artistic features:

> It was built in the style of the Azhar congregational mosque in Cairo. This mosque had a lovely garden to its west, and a cistern . . . [The] decoration is the work of painters from Basra and of the Banu'l-Mu'allim, of whom Kutami and Nazuk are masters.[10]

Durzan commissioned several other buildings, including a pavilion by the Nile. Yet she remained dedicated to the Qarafa mosque. There, she built other public facilities, including a public bathhouse, a large reservoir to provide clean water for drinking and washing, as well as a hydraulic pump to supply water to the ablution hall.

The Last Campaign of al-Aziz

In 985, al-Aziz had celebrated the birth of his son al-Mansur, who would soon be known by his regnal title, *al-Hakim bi-Amr Allah* (the Ruler by the Command of God). Al-Mansur was aged 10 when al-Aziz designated him *wali al-ahd*, and the young prince's succession would come far sooner than many would have imagined.

Reports from Syria alarmed the capital in 995. Led by the emperor Basil II (r. 976–1026), the Byzantine army had returned in full force and had already scored major victories in northern

Syria. As he had done almost two decades earlier, al-Aziz prepared to take to the battlefield.

Preparations for the Fatimid counterattack began in earnest. As battalions were marshalled, al-Aziz set up camp north-east of Cairo. Meanwhile, by the docks, craftsmen laboured to strengthen the Fatimid fleet. Soon, however, disaster struck. On the very day that the newly built ships were to set sail, a major fire engulfed 16 of them and the arsenal (*dar al-sana'a*) in which they were built.

Sectarian rivalries ignited. Gossipmongers blamed a group of Amalfitan merchants, from Italy's southern coast, who were then trading in Fustat; a mob attack resulted in 160 of them being killed. Anti-Christian riots soon spread, and both Melkite and Nestorian churches were plundered. For the Fatimid authorities, the riot was not only an assault on important Mediterranean trading partners, but a flagrant violation of the Imam-caliph's *dhimma*. The rioters were arrested and punished, the surviving merchants were compensated for their losses, and the construction of a new fleet was commissioned.

By the summer of 996, preparations for the expedition to Syria were almost complete. But it was not to be. In August, al-Aziz was struck by a debilitating illness. With the issue of succession now imminent, he summoned the three most senior figures of the realm: the chief judge and *da'i* Muhammad b. al-Nu'man; the tutor and guardian of al-Hakim, al-Ustadh Barjawan; and the veteran general al-Hasan b. Ammar al-Kalbi. To them al-Aziz entrusted the succession and guardianship of al-Hakim before passing away on 14 October 996.

Al-Aziz's final moments with his 11-year-old son were etched in the young prince's memory, as relayed by al-Hakim himself to the historian al-Musabbihi:

> My father summoned me to him just before his death . . . He reached out for me, kissed me, and hugged me closely. He said, 'I am worried for you, O dearest of my heart', and his tears began to flow. Then he [al-Aziz] said, 'Go, O *sayyid* (lord) and play. I am in good health.' So I left, and went to amuse myself with the games young people play, while God, the Exalted and Highest, took al-Aziz away to Himself. Barjawan then hastened to me [while I was] atop a sycamore tree that was in the house, and said, 'Come down, my boy! May God protect you and us all.'
>
> Al-Hakim said: 'When I descended, he placed on my head the turban adorned with jewels, kissed the ground before me and said: "Hail to the Commander of the Faithful, with Almighty God's Mercy and Blessings."'[11]

The Succession of al-Hakim bi-Amr Allah
The accession of an Imam-caliph at such a young age was thus far unprecedented in the Fatimid

dynasty. In Imami Shi'i doctrine, the explicit designation (*nass*) of a child successor was, however, considered apposite, as God's support (*ta'yid*) for His chosen Imam renders the Imam's knowledge and guidance authoritative regardless of age. This was considered as being akin to God enabling Jesus to pronounce his apostleship whilst still an infant in the cradle (Q. 19:29–30). Al-Hakim's youth nonetheless created an opening in the exercise of state power, which many now sought to fill. The rise of the 'servants of state' to the upper echelons of power is a well-known feature of medieval patrimonial polities. It quickly manifested as al-Hakim's reign began.

It was in the army that factionalism became first evident. The military was now principally divided, as often classified in medieval chronicles, between the 'westerners' (*maghariba*), consisting mainly of Kutama Berbers, and the 'easterners' (*mashariqa*), dominated by recently recruited Turkish soldiers. The Kutama had been the backbone of the Fatimid army, their forefathers holding special status as members of the *da'wa* and closely connected (*awliya*) to the Fatimid Imams. During al-Aziz's reign, however, their chieftains had chafed against the challenge to their privilege that arose both from the introduction of the easterners, and from the prominence of Christians and Jews in the administration. They were held in check by al-Aziz, but his sudden demise brought pent up frustrations to the fore.

The Beginnings of Factionalism

At al-Hakim's succession ceremony, one group
was conspicuous by its absence. In the *musalla*
outside Cairo, Kutama chieftains had gathered
to vent their anger and make their demands.
Al-Hasan b. Ammar al-Kalbi, himself a prominent North-African émigré, rode out to negotiate.
In deference, the chiefs pronounced their oath
of allegiance to al-Hakim but only after their
demands were met. Accordingly, the Christian
minister Isa b. Nestorius was dismissed and Ibn
Ammar himself was appointed to the newly
created office of the *wasita* (intermediary), one
akin to that of a vizier.

The return to prominence of the old guard
ignited the first open *maghariba–mashariqa*
conflict. While the Kutama supported Ibn Ammar,
the *mashariqa* rallied around the Turkish Fatimid
general Mangu Tekin, who was then stationed in
Syria. Rivalry turned to open warfare, and the
Kutama subsequently defeated the *mashariqa*
and captured Mangu Tekin, though they eventually released him in honour of his long service to
al-Aziz. The Kutama victory was, however, short-
lived. Riots in Cairo soon compelled Ibn Ammar
to flee. By 997, power thus came to rest in the
hands of al-Ustadh Barjawan – the erstwhile tutor
and guardian of al-Hakim – who now became the
new *wasita*. Both Barjawan and Ibn Ammar
before him ruled as regents, wielding state power
whilst al-Hakim was still in his early teens.

Balancing the privileges of both the *mashariqa*
and the *maghariba*, Barjawan successfully

restored order over the next three years, aided by the Christian official Fahd b. Ibrahim. Barjawan was subsequently accused of neglecting the state administration, but it was his allegedly domineering attitude towards al-Hakim that led to his demise in April 1000; it is said that he was assassinated on the orders of the Imam-caliph.

With Cairo tense in the aftermath of Barjawan's death, al-Hakim addressed the Kutama and Turkish contingents that had gathered in the palace square, instructing them to return home. Five years after his accession, aged 15, al-Hakim was at the helm of affairs.

The Illuminated Mosque

Starting in 990, labourers and craftsmen had toiled for 23 years to build one of Fatimid Cairo's enduring legacies. The *Jami al-Anwar* (Illuminated Mosque), known today as the Mosque of al-Hakim bi-Amr Allah, is over twice the size of al-Azhar, and it inherited structural features from preceding Fatimid mosques. Al-Aziz would often lead prayers there while it was still under construction. Al-Hakim sponsored its completion, and upon its inauguration in 1013, he personally led the prayers there, thus incorporating the mosque into the Fatimid ritual landscape.

When worshippers first approached al-Anwar Mosque, their eyes would have probably been drawn to its towering minarets, one circular and the other square. Upon them were Qur'anic and dedicatory inscriptions carved into stone in ornate Kufic script. On the north minaret, the verse of light (*Ayat al-Nur*, Q. 24:35) was inscribed. On the western minaret, the middle band included the engraving 'The Mercy of God and His blessings be upon you, O *ahl al-bayt*, Surely He is All-Laudable, All-Glorious' (Q. 11:73).

Ornate stonework had not previously been a feature of Egyptian architecture. It is possible that expert artisans from Jerusalem, then a centre of stonemasonry, had been brought to Cairo for the building project, invigorating a new industry in Egypt. Thereon, stonemasonry became a preferred medium for the construction of monumental buildings in the city.

The Fatimid *Da'wa* and the Abbasid Resurgence

In August 1010 in the northern Iraqi city of Mosul, a Friday sermon (*khutba*) was delivered which became imprinted in history. Instead of pronouncing prayers for the Abbasid caliphs, at the command of the city's ruler, the preacher invoked God's blessings on the Fatimid Imam-caliphs from al-Mahdi bi'llah to al-Aziz. The preacher then proclaimed:

> O God, extend all of Your blessings and the most perfect of Your favours to our lord and master, the imam of the age, fortress of the faith, head of the Alid *da'wa* and prophetic religion, Your servant and guardian on Your behalf, al-Mansur Abu Ali al-Hakim bi-Amr Allah, Commander of the Believers, just as You blessed his rightly guided forefathers.[12]

Figure 12. Partial View of the al-Anwar Mosque
View of the upper levels and finial of one of the inner minarets of al-Anwar
Mosque.

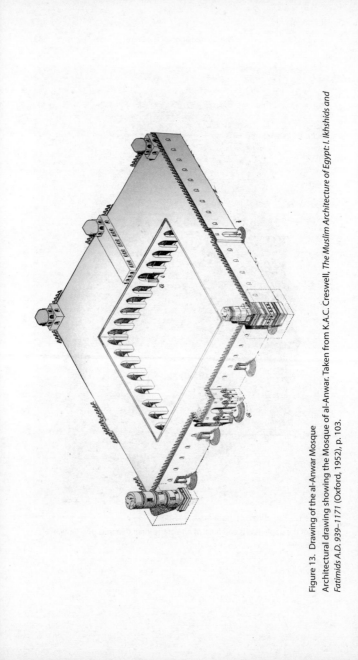

Figure 13. Drawing of the al-Anwar Mosque

Architectural drawing showing the Mosque of al-Anwar. Taken from K.A.C. Creswell, *The Muslim Architecture of Egypt: I. Ikhshids and Fatimids A.D. 939–1171* (Oxford, 1952), p. 103.

Mosul was then ruled by Qirwash b. al-Muqallad (d. 1050), an Arab chieftain of the Banu Uqayl, whose dynasty had Shi'i inclinations but ruled as viceroys of the Abbasid caliph.

The *khutba* of Qirwash, as it came to be known, testified to the increasing growth of the Fatimid *da'wa* and reach of the Fatimid Empire. Three years earlier in Baghdad, during riots between the Shi'i and Sunni communities, the Shi'a had called out the Fatimid Imam-caliph's names, '*ya Hakim ya Mansur*'. Yet until Qirwash's *khutba* of 1010, no major political power in Abbasid heartlands had publicly declared allegiance to the Fatimids. Other cities soon followed suit, and official *khutba*s in al-Hakim's name were pronounced in the Iraqi cities of Anbar, Mada'in (Ctesiphon), and Kufa. This proved short-lived. The Buyid *amir*s, as overlords of the Abbasid caliphs, deployed financial incentives and threat of force to draw Qirwash and others back to the Abbasid fold. The developments, however, highlighted the heightening of Fatimid–Abbasid rivalries in the early 11th century, which had an enduring literary legacy.

Al-Qadir and the Baghdad Manifesto

While the 10th century has been called the 'Shi'i century', the 11th century has been earmarked as the 'Sunni revival'. This period saw the crystallization of the belief that the varied proto-Sunni legal traditions and specific theological schools constituted a single confessional community, that of the *ahl al-sunna wa'l-jama'a* (the people of prophetic tradition and communal consensus). The term denoted the entirety of the Sunni confession. Galvanized by this consolidation, the Abbasid caliphs emerged to present themselves as the symbolic heads of Sunni Islam. Pivotal in cementing this role was the Abbasid caliph, Ahmad b. Ishaq al-Qadir bi'llah (d. 1031). Installed by the Buyids in 991 to be a mere figurehead like his immediate predecessors, al-Qadir used the rapid waning of Buyid power to shore up his own authority over a 40-year-long reign. Casting himself as the spokesman of the Sunni traditions, he emerged at the forefront of efforts to curb the Fatimid political and intellectual advance.

Just over a year after Qirwash's *khutba*, the Abbasid caliph al-Qadir in 1011 issued a proclamation that was read out in Baghdad and several other Iraqi cities. Deriding the Fatimids as impostors and heretics, the proclamation's central claim was that the Fatimids were not the descendants of the Prophet Muhammad. Al-Qadir's document, known today as the 'Baghdad Manifesto', was widely circulated. Over the following centuries, it became ingrained in pro-Abbasid historical writings as the standardized account of the 'false' lineage of the Fatimids. Although some later Sunni scholars, including al-Maqrizi and his teacher Ibn Khaldun, refuted its claims and reaffirmed the Fatimid descent from the Prophet Muhammad, the manifesto continued to be widely reported. For many modern historians of the 19th and early 20th centuries, having access only to a limited number of Arabic medieval texts and almost no Fatimid sources, al-Qadir's document often became the starting point in presenting Fatimid history. Though subsequent historians have since addressed the misrepresentation, the document remains an important artefact of the Abbasid resurgence that coincided with al-Hakim's reign.

Anti-Fatimid works had long proliferated in pro-Abbasid circles. Particularly influential were the writings of the 10th-century figures Ibn Rizam and Akhu Muhsin. Among their allegations were claims that the Fatimids were descendants of a secret society of 'dualists' who feigned being Muslim and aimed to destroy Islam from within. With such works already in circulation, al-Qadir's Baghdad manifesto fell on receptive ears.

Soon thereafter, propaganda degenerated into violence, and in the eastern regions of the Muslim world Ismaili communities bore the heaviest brunt. In the early 11th century, the Ghaznavid ruler Mahmud b. Sebuk Tegin (d. 1030) was on campaign in the Indian subcontinent. Ardent to demonstrate his credentials as a supporter of al-Qadir, he attacked the Fatimid Ismaili principality of Multan in Sindh. Proclaiming the Ismailis as deviants (*mulhid*), he unleashed a massacre. A precedent had been set, and further bloody massacres of Ismailis in Iran and North Africa were soon to follow.

Approaches to the Reign of al-Hakim bi-Amr Allah

More than any other Fatimid sovereign, the Imam-caliph al-Hakim has been the subject of commentary by modern historians. His presentation in the surviving medieval sources has led to his reign being considered enigmatic at best, or cruel and tyrannical at worst. Several factors contributed to this assessment, including the nature of his personality, his deification by the Druze religious movement that emerged from elements within the Fatimid *da'wa*, and the ambivalence in the sources regarding his disappearance and death in 1021. Over time, the allure of the dramatic has meant that presentations of al-Hakim have pervaded popular literature.

Many 19th- and early 20th-century historians accentuated the cruelty of al-Hakim, based on medieval chronicles that were often hostile to the Fatimids. His reputed transgressions include the execution of numerous state officials, the issuing of edicts restricting the public activities of women, the banning of specific foodstuffs, the proscription of Sunni subjects, and the public cursing of the first three caliphs. Such histories highlighted the persecution of Christians and Jews by al-Hakim, whose policies were presented as being in stark contrast to those of his father and grandfather. These included the obligation for Christians and Jews to wear distinctive attire, the banning of public Christian processions, and the pillaging and destruction of churches culminating in the razing of the Church of the Holy Sepulchre in

Jerusalem in 1009. The latter is often cited as a catalyst for the unleashing of the Crusades later in the century.

Across these works a significant paradox prevails, however, as reflected in the medieval sources. These relay images of a benevolent sovereign, concerned with the welfare of the poor and the needy. They convey accounts of al-Hakim's asceticism, his eschewal of wealth and luxury, and his resolute sense of justice. They recount the succour he provided the starving during years of crippling famine, and his generous distribution of money and land to the most stricken. The sources also recount al-Hakim's policies of granting personal access to the people, his listening to petitions in person, and his insistence on state officials granting justice to those who sought it. The reports culminate in attestations of al-Hakim's favour amongst the general populace, with eulogies by Jewish writers extolling his sense of justice.

Despite the potency of the contrasting images of al-Hakim, 20th-century histories often expressed a reluctance, with some important exceptions, to critically assess the contradictory reports concerning his biography, to separate reliable accounts from myths and legend, and identify stereotypes and tropes, as is a requisite in any historical survey of the past.

In recent decades, scholarship has progressed to more nuanced assessments. Critical explanations proffered by historians include understanding the economic rationalizations of al-Hakim's banning of some agricultural produce. Others contextualize his dealings with state officials as rooted in 'patrimonial polities', with the Imam-caliph seeking to prevent the takeover of the state by its elites. Similarly, the rise of messianic movements centred on Jerusalem is suggested for understanding the destruction and subsequent rebuilding of the Church of the Holy Sepulchre.

It is increasingly evident now that presentations of al-Hakim are highly dependent on critical readings of the existing sources, including both sympathetic and hostile accounts. It is apparent that aspects of al-Hakim's rule were considered enigmatic even among his Ismaili followers, with Fatimid *daʿwa* literature seeking to understand the atypical features of his reign. However, al-Hakim's rule largely coincided with that of the Abbasid al-Qadir and would have almost certainly been impacted by the burgeoning anti-Ismaili literature. As historians have now recognized, hostile propaganda and patent fabrications about al-Hakim were circulated and became enmeshed in the historical record, with fact and legend often interwoven. Aside from fanciful fabrications, a more nuanced case in point is the widely reported claim that in 1004 al-Hakim ordered curses against companions of the Prophet to be inscribed on the outer walls of mosques and marketplaces, before ordering their erasure years later. Though some 20th-century historians disputed the veracity of the claim, it was often reproduced by subsequent historians. More recent scholarship demonstrates, based on the accounts of al-Maqrizi, Ibn Khaldun, and Idris Imad al-Din, that such claims are no longer wholly reliable. The contextual, source-critical studies of al-Hakim and his reign remain a work in progress.

Chapter 5

Science and Scholarship in the City Victorious

As the Fatimid Empire prospered, Cairo emerged as a major centre of cultural and intellectual efflorescence. Institutions of learning flourished, and with patronage and opportunity abounding, scholars, scientists, artists, and architects came to the Fatimid capital. Cairo also served as the heartbeat of the Fatimid *da'wa*: *da'i*s came to study, teach, and write, leading to the production of some of the most influential works of Fatimid doctrine and philosophy.

Towards a Knowledge Society

The Fatimid arrival in 969 had brought a new impetus to a culture of learning that had already animated Egypt in past centuries through the efforts of Coptic bishops, Jewish rabbis, and Muslim *ulama*. Al-Mu'izz's arrival brought a renewal of public debates (*munazara*s) among scholars of different specializations and confessions; these became a feature of Fatimid courtly life. Thereafter, the vizier Ya'qub b. Killis gained renown for his patronage of learned figures, with judges, jurists, Qur'an reciters, and grammarians being a regular presence in his audience. But it was the sustained patronage of learning that particularly invigorated Cairo's new culture of scholarship.

Al-Azhar had served as Cairo's principal congregational mosque since its inception. In al-Aziz's reign, the extension of caliphal patronage in the year 988 saw the beginnings of its millennia-long history as a centre of scholarship:

> The vizier Abu'l-Faraj Ya'qub ibn Killis asked the caliph al-Aziz bi'llah to specify the salaries for a few jurists. Thereupon, the caliph granted each of them a sufficient salary. He ordered a piece of land to be bought and a house to be built next to the Azhar Mosque. Each Friday they assembled in the mosque and formed [study] circles after the [midday]* prayer until the time for the afternoon prayer . . . Their number was thirty-five.[1]

The provision earmarked al-Azhar as a space of learning for law and jurisprudence. The mosque would also become a site of one of the preeminent methods of knowledge dissemination in the Fatimid milieu, that of the *majalis*. Among the earliest features of the Fatimid *da'wa* were the *majalis al-hikma* (the sessions of wisdom) – lectures and study sessions delivered by *da'i*s to the Ismaili faithful. Utilised during the *dawr al-satr* as conduits for conveying the teachings of the Ismaili Imams, they had initially been held behind closed doors or in open fields. In Fatimid Ifriqiya, the *majalis* took place in the Imam-caliph's palaces, and in Cairo the practice continued at both the Eastern Palace and the al-Azhar Mosque. As the authoritative guide in doctrine, the Imam-caliph would formally approve the content of the *majalis*. Over time, the practice developed where the texts of the *majalis* bore an Imam-caliph's seal to signify his approval of their contents. In al-Hakim's time, al-Musabbihi recounts:

> The *da'i* used to hold continuous sessions in the palace to read what was read to the saintly [*al-awliya*, 'the initiates'] and [collect] the dues connected with it. [The *da'i*]* would hold a separate session for the *awliya*; another for the courtiers [*al-khassa*]* and high officials as well as those attached to the palaces as servants or in other capacities; a further session for the simple people and strangers in the city; a separate session for women in the Mosque of Qahira called al-Azhar; and a session for the wives ... and the noble women of the palaces.[2]

The House of Knowledge
Patronage of scholarship received a major impetus in 1005, when al-Hakim founded the famous House of Knowledge (*Dar al-Ilm*) in Cairo. With funding provided for the buildings and its operations, stipends for scholars, and its opening to the public, the Dar al-Ilm marked another milestone in the institutionalization of education in the medieval Muslim world. Central to its function was the provision of books brought

over from the palace library, as recounted by al-Musabbihi:

> On this Saturday [in March] . . . the so-called House of Knowledge in Cairo was inaugurated. The jurists took up residence there, and the books from the palace libraries were moved into it . . . lectures were held there by the Qur'an readers, astronomers, grammarians, and philologists, as well as physicians. . . .
>
> Into this house they brought all the books that the commander of the faithful al-Hakim bi-Amr Allah ordered to bring there, that is, the manuscripts in all the domains of science and culture, to an extent to which they had never been brought together for a prince. He allowed access to all this to people of all walks of life, whether they wanted to read books or dip into them. One of the already mentioned blessings, the likes of which had been unheard of, was also that he granted substantial salaries to all those who were appointed by him there to do service – jurists and others. People from all walks of life visited the House; some came to read books, others to copy them, and yet others to study. He [al-Hakim] also donated what people needed: ink, writing reeds, paper, and inkstands.[3]

Books had long been cherished by al-Hakim's predecessors, and by al-Aziz's time Fatimid palace libraries contained some of the finest works of their age. Amongst them, chroniclers recount,

were autographed copies of the *Kitab al-Ayn* by
the famed grammarian Khalil b. Ahmad (d. 786),
the history of the seminal historian al-Tabari
(d. 923), and the works of the great lexicographer
Ibn Durayd (d. ca. 933).

The Dar al-Ilm was initially funded through
the state treasury, but in 1010 al-Hakim established a *waqf* (endowment) for its upkeep by
dedicating to it a portion of the rent from his
estates in Fustat. Al-Maqrizi's rendition of the
waqf's expenses provides a rare insight into the
Dar al-Ilm's day-to-day functioning:

> For the purchase of mats and other household
> effects, 10 dinars; for paper for the scribe, i.e.
> the copyist, 90 dinars . . . for the librarian 48
> dinars; for the purchase of water 12; for the
> servant 15; for paper, ink and writing reeds for
> the scholars studying there 12; for repairing
> the curtains 1 dinar; for the repair of possibly
> torn books or loose leaves 12; for the purchase
> of felt for blankets in the winter 5; for the
> purchase of carpets in the winter 4 dinars.[4]

The Scientists of Cairo

In the early 1000s, upon the Muqattam cliffs
overlooking the capital, the astronomer Ibn
Yunus may have often been found with his gaze
turned skywards. Well known in his lifetime,
today Ibn Yunus is counted among the medieval
world's most prominent astronomers, whose
career testified to the thriving intellectual élan
of his age.

A native of Egypt, Ali b. Abd al-Rahman b. Ahmad b. Yunus was born into a family of noted scholars. Distinguished already in his role as a legal witness (*adl*), it was as an astronomer that Ibn Yunus came to be remembered. In 990, the Imam-caliph al-Aziz commissioned Ibn Yunus to prepare an updated astronomical handbook, known as a *zij* in Arabic. Such works charted the position of the sun in relation to the constellation of planets and stars and determined the times of sunrise and sunset. They came to be used by people in many professions, from sailors to those who called the faithful to prayer. While a number were already in circulation, including the *zij* of the Abbasid caliph al-Ma'mun (r. 818–33), many had become dated.

By 1003, Ibn Yunus completed his magisterial work. Dedicated to al-Hakim, the *al-Zij al-Hakimi* began with tables of Ibn Yunus's own observations and his critiques of the findings of earlier astronomers. Thereafter, he included his own findings on solar and lunar eclipses and equinoxes, and hundreds of formulae on spherical astronomy. The work remained famous for several centuries. Two hundred years later, the renowned Egyptian biographer Ibn Khallikan wrote: 'I have seen a copy in four volumes . . . I have seen many works containing astronomical tables, but never met with one so full as this.'[5]

In April 1006, the SN1006 supernova erupted across the night sky. Today, it is described as perhaps the brightest cosmic event witnessed in human history. Appearing low on the southern horizon, its red hues are said to have coloured the nights over many months. Monks from Switzerland to chroniclers in China reported the event. One of the most detailed accounts, however, comes from the work of another up-and-coming scholar of Fatimid Cairo.

Ali b. Ridwan was around 19 years old when the supernova appeared. He was the son of a baker and was born in Giza. His autobiography describes his poverty-stricken early years and his impulse towards learning the sciences, especially medicine and astronomy. The self-taught scholar would become a prodigy. Amongst his works was a commentary on the *Tetrabiblos* of the eminent Alexandrian scholar Ptolemy (d. ca. 168). In the commentary, Ibn Ridwan detailed the appearance of SN1006, a phenomenon whose remnants were only fully identified in 1965. Aged 32, around 1019, Ibn Ridwan's own career reached a milestone with his appointment as the personal physician of al-Hakim.

A host of other contemporaries pursued the study of sciences in Fatimid Cairo. The famed historian Mukhtar al-Musabbihi was noted to have written works on astrology. A Jewish scholar at the court of al-Hakim known simply as al-Isra'ili composed works on the 'Sciences of the Stars'. But perhaps the most famous of all was Ibn al-Haytham, the luminary of the age in the science of optics.

Born in Basra in 965, al-Hasan b. al-Haytham grew up and studied in Baghdad. With peer jealousy hampering his advancement at the Abbasid court, Ibn al-Haytham migrated to Cairo during al-Hakim's reign. There, he sought out the Fatimid ruler to propose an audacious plan – an engineering project that would alter the course of the Nile and regulate its cycles. Though considerable effort was expended, it remained, however, unsuccessful. Only over a millennium later in the 1960s was the Nile successfully dammed, remaining among Egypt's most expensive infrastructural projects to date. Following the failed attempt, Ibn al-Haytham left Cairo fearing severe reprisal. Yet Cairo remained an intellectual magnet, and Ibn Haytham would return in the reign of al-Hakim's grandson, al-Mustansir bi'llah.

Ibn al-Haytham's scholarship was prodigious: he wrote over 100 works on mathematics, astronomy, and physics, only half of which survive today. It was in optics that Ibn al-Haytham made his ground-breaking discovery. For centuries prior, scholars believed the human eye emitted rays that allowed the viewing of objects. Through experimentation, Ibn al-Haytham proved instead that it was external light which enters the eye. To verify his theory, he used a darkened room that allowed light to enter through a tiny hole, and which projected an image of the outside world onto the backwall of the room. Hence was born the 'camera obscura', literally a 'darkened room'. The discovery had critical implications for the evolution of Islamic architecture, and centuries later, after Ibn al-Haytham's work was translated into Latin with the title 'Perspective', its influence resounded through the discovery of

Figure 14. Ibn al-Haytham on Iraqi Banknote
This Iraqi banknote depicting Ibn al-Haytham was in use from 1980 to 2003.

'perspective' in painting and architecture during the Renaissance.

The Fatimid *Da'wa* in the New Millennium

The flourishing of Cairo as a major centre of learning was complemented by the arrival of Ismaili *da'i*s to the capital, particularly from the eastern regions of the Muslim world. By the early 11th century, two became especially noteworthy for their prominence and scholarship – Ahmad b. Ibrahim al-Nisaburi and Hamid al-Din al-Kirmani.

Da'i *al-Nisaburi and the Code of Conduct*

While little is known about Ahmad b. Ibrahim al-Nisaburi's personal life, the *da'i* was probably originally from Nishapur, then a thriving metropolis in Khurasan, eastern Iran. After his arrival in Cairo, seemingly during al-Aziz's reign, he made his mark by composing several important works that survive today. In his *Kitab Istitar*

Figure 15. Frontispiece of *Selenographia*

Selenographia, sive Lunae descriptio ('Selenography, or A Description of the Moon'), by Johannes Hevelius, was printed in 1647. Its frontispiece depicts Ibn al-Haytham on the left and Galileo (in Middle Eastern dress) on the right, possibly symbolizing the intertwining of later Western science with earlier Eastern scientific discoveries.

al-imam ('Book on the Concealment of the Imam'), al-Nisaburi relates a history of the Ismaili *da'wa* during the *dawr al-satr*, recounting the journey of al-Mahdi bi'llah from Syria to Ifriqiya. The vivid account suggests that he had access to first-hand sources and may well have conferred with descendants of the founding figures of the Fatimid *da'wa*. The work remains a vital chronicle today for reconstructing the earliest periods of Fatimid history.

In the later years of al-Hakim's reign, al-Nisaburi composed a code of conduct for the *da'wa*. Titled *al-Risala al-mujaza al-kafiya fi adab al-du'at* ('A Brief Treatise on the Code of Conduct of *Da'is*'), it set out the qualifications, responsibilities, and moral outlook expected of *da'is*.

Since its earliest decades, the Fatimid *da'wa* had been hierarchically organized: each *da'i* reported to a superior, with the highest rank being that of the chief *da'i* (*da'i al-du'at*, lit. the *da'i* of *da'is*) who were under the leadership of the Imam. Yet by the 11th century the *da'wa* organization extended from Ifriqiya to Central Asia and Sindh, and vast distances meant regional *da'is* were afforded significant autonomy and responsibility. In their localities, *da'is* served not only as representatives of the Imam, but also as community leaders responsible for the well-being of the believers. Texts of 'codes of conduct' delineating their required qualifications and characteristics, were central in defining their role.

Al-Nisaburi's 'Code of Conduct' drew on the popular genre of *adab* manuals in Arabic literature and built on earlier works, including an earlier 'code of conduct' composed by Qadi al-Nu'man. In his work, al-Nisaburi set out the leadership qualities of an ideal *da'i*:

> Thus a *da'i* should possess all of the virtues that are found separately among the rest of the people . . . There should be in him the qualities of those who administer the government, among the virtues of which are courage, generosity, skill in management, prudence, political aptitude and cultural refinements . . . He must also possess the qualifications of the physicians, their solicitude, and their careful ministration to the sick, for he is the doctor of souls . . . He is the guiding pilot through the desert and the hard steppe on the dark night; it is he who guides to the straight path and to the proper way.[6]

Such manuals were especially pertinent in hostile lands where the home of the local *da'i* served as a haven for the community. There the *majalis* would be held, and there the believers would gather on special occasions as well as to seek guidance and support. The *da'i*s were also required to mediate on personal as well as communal issues, and they were entrusted with the collection and delivery of the believers' religious dues and offerings to the Imam. For al-Nisaburi, however, it was the *da'i*'s role as a teacher that was paramount. He emphasized that through teaching, new adherents were brought

into the fold, and he believed that *da'is* needed
to master a range of religious sciences, including
understandings of the Qur'an and the teachings
of the Prophets and the Imams.

Da'i *al-Kirmani and the Lamps of the Imamate*

A luminary of the Fatimid *da'wa*, Hamid al-Din
al-Kirmani was unrivalled in the Ismaili philosophical tradition. Like al-Nisaburi, however,
little is known about his life. Originating from
Kirman in south-eastern Iran, he lived initially
in Iraq, where much of his intellectual formation took shape.

Al-Kirmani was well read in the Qur'an, *hadith*,
and *tafsir* (Qur'anic exegesis), Muslim history and
law, and literature and lexicography. He would
have studied foundational Shi'i and Ismaili texts,
including the writings of the Ismaili *da'is* of
previous generations like Abu Hatim al-Razi
(d. 933/934), Muhammad al-Nasafi (d. 943), Abu
Ya'qub al-Sijistani (d. after 971), Ja'far b. Mansur
al-Yaman (who died during the reign of al-Mu'izz),
and Qadi al-Nu'man. Al-Kirmani would have also
studied the works of earlier Muslim philosophers,
as well as of those of the classical Greek tradition
at a time when the bookshops in Baghdad were
well stocked with their writings. In his own writings, al-Kirmani drew from this vast repertoire, his
breadth of expertise evident in his quoting of the
ancient scriptures, using Hebrew from the Torah
and Syriac from the Gospels.

It was as a philosopher that al-Kirmani was to
have the greatest influence. Rejecting the claim

that it was possible to achieve goodness by reason alone and that humans required no divine guidance, al-Kirmani emphasized the necessity of seeking knowledge and guidance from the divinely inspired figure of the Fatimid Imam. Amongst his most influential works was the *Masabih fi ithbat al-imama* ('The Lamps that Establish the Imamate'), which presented rational proofs for the necessity of the imamate and reiterated the universal authority and lineage of the Imam-caliph al-Hakim:

> He is from the offspring of prophecy and is a descendant of al-Husayn . . . He has been designated by pure forefathers through Ali b. Abi Talib to Muhammad, the Chosen.[7]

Writing in Iraq at a time when al-Qadir's anti-Fatimid efforts were intensifying, al-Kirmani dedicated the work to Fakhr al-Mulk (d. 1016), a Buyid governor of Baghdad known for his affinity to the *ahl al-bayt*. Al-Kirmani's towering scholarship earned him the prestigious title *Hujjat al-Iraqayn* ('the Proof of the Two Iraqs', referring to Iraq and western Iran). Then, probably at the request of the Fatimid chief *da'i*, al-Kirmani was summoned to Cairo, where particular challenges awaited.

The Emergence of the Druze Movement

Al-Kirmani arrived in Cairo sometime in 1015 amidst unprecedented times. A splinter group from within the Ismaili *da'wa* had emerged.

Their controversial doctrines had galvanized opposition from both the official Ismaili *da'wa* and Egypt's Sunni populace.

The movement that came to be labelled as the Druze movement began in the last decade of al-Hakim's reign. While its early developments remain opaque, it is known that dissident *da'is*, including Hamza b. Ali (d. 1021), Muhammad b. Ismail al-Darazi (d. 1018), and al-Akhram (d. 1018), were amongst the movement's leading figures. All three most likely originated from eastern Iran and Khurasan, where Neoplatonic notions of creation and emanation had deep roots. In consonance with messianic beliefs regarding divine guides, the dissident *da'is* began preaching that the era of Islam had ended, and that Imam al-Hakim had transcended the imamate and was a locus of divinity. Al-Darazi is said to have been executed for his preaching and was ostracized by other Druze leaders, including Hamza b. Ali. However, his name remained attached to the movement, as it is from where the term 'Druze' derives.

In response to the Druze, a hostile reaction ensued, including that led by the then Fatimid chief *da'i*, Khatkin al-Dayf. Violent riots erupted amongst the Sunni communities in Fustat as the dissident preachers became increasingly public. With some supporters of the movement targeted and others killed, the leaders of the Druze movement fled Egypt and sought refuge in the mountainous regions of Syria and Lebanon, which remain the Druze homeland to the present day.

The *da'i* al-Kirmani emerged at the forefront in articulating the Fatimid *da'wa*'s official response. In his *Mabasim al-bisharat* ('Mouths of Happy Tidings'), al-Kirmani refuted the Druze belief that al-Hakim was the last Imam and, instead, affirmed the continuity of the imamate in perpetuity. In contextualizing al-Hakim's seemingly paradoxical rulings, al-Kirmani argued the incumbency of knowing that although the Imams each had their own policies and teachings, and each acted according to their specific parameters and circumstances, all together they formed a chain in the 'rope of God' (*habli'llah*) – a continuous line of Imams. The *da'i* noted that as conditions changed with each generation, it was the living Imam's prerogative to act according to that change. He explained that because al-Hakim's reign did not enjoy the same safety and stability as that of his grandfather, al-Mu'izz, it required different responses that were not always understood – extraordinary times called for extraordinary measures.

The Druze controversy receded over the following years. In time, al-Kirmani's homeland beckoned. On returning to Iraq, al-Kirmani composed his most important philosophical treatise, *Rahat al-aql* ('Comfort of Reason'), earmarking him as amongst the most prolific Ismaili *da'i*s of his time.

Turmoil and Restoration of Order
Al-Hakim's 25-year reign saw turmoil both in Egypt and in the broader Muslim world. In the

middle years of his rule, war and scarcity ravaged the country. Earlier, in 1004, a major rebellion against the Fatimids erupted among the Bedouin tribes of the Libyan provinces. The revolt was led by Abu Rakwa who styled himself 'caliph', though his claim to descent from the Andalusian Umayyad caliphs was disputed. Abu Rakwa inflicted major defeats on Fatimid armies on his march to Alexandria and then to Giza. It was only in 1006, in Fayyum, that Abu Rakwa was decisively defeated, and he was executed a year later.

The strife that had erupted was exacerbated by famine. Recurrent low rises of the Nile from 1004 to 1007 saw agricultural production plummet, with hunger following in its wake. In response, al-Hakim repeatedly ordered measures to compel suppliers to make grain available to the millers and bakers. The strained circumstances heightened Shi'i–Sunni conflict within the capital, mirroring sectarian conflict in Baghdad over the same years. This climate also served as the backdrop to the reports about al-Hakim's initial ordinances against Christians and Jews, with accounts relating the demolition of churches and proscriptions on their public life, culminating in the destruction of the Church of the Holy Sepulchre in 1009. The same period also saw the Fatimid imposition of strict social codes, including those restricting the mobility of women in public spaces. Historians have examined such trends as a backdrop from which to understand the appearance of Abu Rakwa, the destruction of the churches, and the appearance of the Druze in the following decade.

By the second decade of the 1000s, however, the Nile returned to its normal levels, and as stability displaced scarcity, a broader restoration of social order and prosperity followed. In 1008, al-Hakim issued his famous edict to ease sectarian tensions, especially amongst the Sunni and Shiʻi populace. In it, he pronounced the Qur'anic injunction that sought to negate the forced imposition of doctrines, and he appealed to a diversity of interpretations. A version of the edict was recorded by Ibn Khaldun:

> The Commander of the Believers [al-Hakim] recites to you the verses from the Clear Book of God, 'There is no compulsion in religion: true guidance has become distinct from error, so whoever rejects false gods and believes in God has grasped the firmest handhold, one that will never break. God is all hearing and all knowing' (Q. 2:256) . . . To each Muslim there is his own reasoning in religion, and each will return to God.[8]

The decree also reiterated the legal and performative rights of various Muslim communities. In the final years of al-Hakim's reign, the strictures against Christian and Jewish communities were similarly eased.

The Demise of al-Hakim and the Rise of Sitt al-Mulk

Among the widely reported features of al-Hakim's biography was his turn to an ascetic lifestyle in his final years. During this time, the Imam-caliph seemingly eschewed the allure of courtly life, opting for simplicity and solitude. The Muqattam hills became a favoured retreat, and there al-Hakim often rode accompanied by only a handful of trusted figures. It was on one such nocturnal outing on 13 February 1021 that al-Hakim rode out to the hills, never to return. Varying accounts relay that his wounded mule and a bloodied shirt were all that were recovered.

Perhaps more than any other incident, the disappearance and death of al-Hakim have contributed to the enigma surrounding his life. Medieval sources became rife with innuendo as different rumours circulated about the nature of his demise. Some claimed robbery and murder, others laid blame on his sister, Sitt al-Mulk, alongside other sordid accusations, whilst yet others spoke of personal vengeance. One version that gained currency in Cairo and Fustat was that al-Hakim had not died, but, weary of public life, had migrated to Basra or another eastern city. For decades afterwards, individuals appeared in Egypt claiming that they were al-Hakim, and often attracted support.

It was at this moment of crisis that one of the most remarkable women of Muslim history came to the fore. When news of al-Hakim's disappearance arrived at the palace, it was first conveyed to his sister Sitt al-Mulk. Behind palace walls, apprehension prevailed as a void in power loomed. Three months later a resolution emerged.

Earlier in 1005, the Fatimid household had celebrated the birth of a new prince. Ali, the young son of al-Hakim, would subsequently reign with the title *al-Zahir li-I'zaz Din Allah* (He who Appears Openly to Glorify the Religion of God). The new prince had a distinct Fatimid maternal lineage, born from the union of al-Hakim and Amina, daughter of Abd Allah (the son of al-Mu'izz). On the Eid al-Adha that followed al-Hakim's disappearance, al-Zahir – now 16 years old – was proclaimed the next Fatimid Imam-caliph.

The securing of al-Zahir's succession was complex. During his reign, al-Hakim reputedly appointed two successors from the line of his cousins in descent from al-Mahdi bi'llah: one as *wali ahd al-muslimin* (the heir apparent of the Muslims) and the other as *wali ahd al-mu'minin* (the heir apparent of the Faithful). Whether these were meant to be his actual successors in a model that separated the spiritual imamate from the temporal caliphate or whether they were meant to be temporary placeholders safeguarding the imamate during al-Zahir's early years remains debated. With Imami Shi'i doctrine upholding the continuity of the imamate in the direct line of the Imam's male descent as a central tenet, the expectation prevailed that the imamate would pass onto al-Hakim's son.

In the intervening months between al-Hakim's disappearance and al-Zahir's succession, it was Sitt al-Mulk who ensured that the power brokers of the empire fell in line behind the young

Imam-caliph. For the next two years, *al-Sayyida al-Amma* (the Princess-Aunt) served as the regent of the empire.

That Sitt al-Mulk was a remarkable woman of her age was acknowledged by her contemporaries and by later Muslim historians. Yet medieval portrayals of Sitt al-Mulk are at times contradictory, and often patriarchal. Some medieval historians were eager to charge her with her brother's murder and posit accusations, including inappropriate relations with men, but other notable historians like Ibn al-Dawadari and Ibn Taghribirdi defended her probity and virtue. The question of how medieval accounts on Sitt al-Mulk were shaped by later chroniclers' bias towards a woman's involvement in the political arena remain, however, to be systematically studied.

Sitt al-Mulk's ascent as regent of the empire perhaps best epitomizes the legacy of her foremothers: her grandmother Durzan Taghrid and her own mother al-Sayyida al-Aziziyya; both paved the path for Fatimid women by patronizing public works. Nonetheless, Sitt al-Mulk's stature and accomplishments were unprecedented.

The Western Palace of Cairo – Sitt al-Mulk's home – was a locus of power and patronage. As inheritors of family wealth, the women of the Fatimid household often oversaw the development of their own private offices, also known as *diwan*s, to manage their properties and incomes. These were often staffed by figures who would themselves later ascend through the government administration, with the support of their patron. During al-Hakim's early reign, there is little mention of his interactions with Sitt al-Mulk, apart from an occasional exchange of courtly gifts. Once al-Hakim assumed the reins of power, however, the sources note that the young caliph would consult with his elder sister, while also attempting to keep her growing power in check. Meanwhile, Sitt al-Mulk's patronage of a vast network of merchants and officials empowered her to gauge shifts of power across the empire, and to forewarn the Imam-caliph accordingly. Thereafter, the royal princess became a stalwart of the Fatimid household, acting as guardian to al-Zahir and supporting his mother, Amina. During her two-year regency, Sitt al-Mulk was at the helm of the Fatimid administration. In 1023, she passed away, aged 53. The statement by the chronicler Ibn Hammad offers a befitting obituary: 'She supported the empire and upheld it.'[9]

Chapter 6

The Empire of the Seas

From their beginnings in Ifriqiya to the high-point of empire in Egypt, the Mediterranean Sea was integral to the Fatimids' venture. As their fleets sailed from Sicily to Syria, their trading networks flourished following the gradual westward shift of commercial enterprise from Iraq towards Egypt and Ifriqiya. In the 11th century, the empire's maritime influence would extend from the Red Sea to the Indian Ocean and beyond, interlinking ports from Yemen and East Africa to India and China. The burgeoning commercial enterprise often went hand in glove with the spread of the Fatimid *da'wa*.

The Fatimid Mapmaker

Sometime between 1020 and 1050, an exceptional work titled 'The Book of Curiosities of the Sciences and Marvels for the Eye' (*Kitab Ghara'ib al-funun wa-mulah al-uyun*) was composed. Its author appears to have been closely connected to the Fatimid *dawla* and *da'wa*. Visually striking, the book is replete with intricately coloured maps, diagrams, and drawings; proficient cartography suggests the author's background as a mapmaker. A rectangular world map found within combines

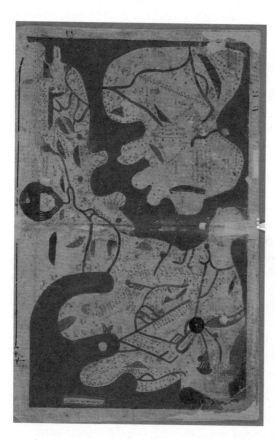

Figure 16. Map of the World from *Kitab Ghara 'ib al-funun*

The anonymous *Kitab Ghara 'ib al-funun* was first compiled in Egypt between 1020 and 1050. The map shown here is from an incomplete copy, probably made in Egypt in the late 12th or early 13th century. The manuscript contains many unique maps, illustrations, and rare texts.

the cartographic traditions of late antiquity and the Muslim world, and it provides the earliest use of a scale bar (to provide latitudes) found in any surviving map from the Muslim world or Western Europe. The recent discovery of the *Book of Curiosities*, and its painstaking analysis by historians, has significantly deepened our understanding of the Fatimid maritime landscape.[1]

In the introduction to the work, the stated objective is to examine the principles that animate the skies ('the raised-up roof') and the earth ('the laid-down bed'). The sources used demonstrate the interconnectedness of the author's world. When discussing the universe, the author deploys astronomical systems of late antiquity and star systems of Arab nomads and demonstrates knowledge of the astronomical systems and centres of learning in India. For the description of winds, the work relies on the discourses of the Christian Copts of Egypt and displays a similar breadth of knowledge in the descriptions of the earth.

A striking feature of the *Book of Curiosities* is its attentiveness to water. Detailed visual representations of oceans and lakes, including those in Africa and Central Asia, are accompanied by maps of major riverways, including the Oxus and Indus rivers. It also provides one of the most accurate understandings of the Nile River system recorded in Muslim scholarship until the modern age, sourced notably from Coptic informants:

> The largest lake on the face of the Earth is the lake known as the Marsh (*al-batiha*) on the

equator, which is the source of the Nile and its floods . . . It has a mountain that is covered with snow during winter and summer. Most Copts maintain that the Sun, when in the summer is at its zenith over this mountain, melts the snow away and causes the rise of the Nile and its continuous flow.[2]

The Fatimid Seafaring World

The first Fatimid capital, al-Mahdiyya, was built as a port-city on the Mediterranean, enabling Fatimid fleets to establish a powerful naval and commercial presence. Thereafter, Fatimid Sicily emerged as a vital economic hub: Palermo was a thriving trading port under its Kalbid governors and the island's woodlands provided much-needed timber for the navy.

During al-Muʿizz's reign especially, naval power had been central to the Fatimid consolidation of power, particularly in the conflicts against the Umayyads of Andalusia and the Byzantines in Sicily and Italy between 955 and 965. Following their entry into Egypt, the navy was pivotal in securing Fatimid control over the Syrian coastland. While naval warfare between Mediterranean powers took place intermittently, these were punctuated by long periods of peace, fostering a lively culture of social and economic interaction across the Mediterranean basin.

For dockworkers at the Egyptian ports of Alexandria, Damietta, and Cairo, these exchanges would have resulted in a hive of activity. Onto departing vessels, they would load an array of goods, including flax, sugarcane, dyes, glass, ceramic wares, gold, spices, silk, other textiles, and artisanal goods. From disembarking Italian and Byzantine vessels, they would unload commodities that were in high demand in Fatimid lands, including iron, wood, wheat, and cheese.

Certain trunk routes became well established, with one prominent itinerary being Alexandria – al-Mahdiyya – Palermo – Alexandria, a journey usually lasting from spring to autumn. To the west, a shorter route sailed from Tinnis in Egypt to Ascalon and other Syrian ports, while several other sea routes were also active. Across all these ventures, Cairo and Fustat served as major entrepôts.

The Glass Wreck
Around 1025 a small but heavily laden ship arrived at a cove known today as Serçe Limanı, close to the present-day city of Marmaris on Turkey's Anatolian coast. Dashed against the rocks, however, the ship and its contents were dragged to the bottom of the sea. The fate of the sailors is unknown. The wreckage lay undisturbed for nearly a thousand years until in the late 1970s divers began recovering the remains.

The Serçe Limanı wreck was most likely a Byzantine merchant vessel returning from the Fatimid ports in Syria. Among the items recovered from the seabed were amphoras, glazed plates and bowls, ceramic jugs and vessels, and gold jewellery. Included also were large quantities of

Figure 17. Fatimid Jewellery
Three pendants and a ring from the Fatimid period. These are examples of the
type of jewellery that would have been transported by the ship wrecked at
Serçe Limanı.

Figure 18. Fatimid-Era Glass Bottle
A glass bottle similar to the ones found on the Serçe Limanı shipwreck.

glassware, consisting of glass bottles, glass lamps, and sackfuls of broken glass, probably intended to be taken to Constantinople for reuse. It was these that led to the ship being called 'The Glass Wreck'. The products probably originated in Syria and Palestine where, by the 11th century, the makers of glass (*zujaj*) were famed for their craftsmanship – their profession being amongst many that thrived on maritime trade.

These worlds of maritime interaction are represented in a distinct map of the Mediterranean found in the *Book of Curiosities*. It locates all the major ports and islands and includes information such as the availability of fresh water, the size of harbours and anchorages, locations of fortifications, and wind directions. The inland features of the shores are presented from an ocean-faring gaze – from the vantage point of a sailor looking onto land.

Among the distinctive features of the *Book of Curiosities* are maps of port-cities such as al-Mahdiyya and Palermo. Graphically showcasing their grand structures and fortifications, they accentuate imperial power and reflect the vantage point of Fatimid officials. Also included is a map of Tinnis, a now abandoned port-city on the south-eastern corner of the Mediterranean that once was a bastion of industry and trade.

Tinnis: The City of Five Thousand Looms

Sometime in the early 11th century, in the Egyptian city of Tinnis, Shihab al-Din Ahmad b. Muhammad – commonly known as Ibn Bassam

– set out for his day's work. A writer and scholar who had memorized the Qur'an, Ibn Bassam was the city's main market inspector (*muhtasib*), an office which by then had a long and important function in Muslim statecraft, and about which Ibn Bassam would come to write a manual. As a scholar, Ibn Bassam also penned a history of Tinnis itself, providing a lively account of life in a major Fatimid port-city. A bustling city of around 50,000 people, Tinnis was then an important trading port between Egypt and the Syrian–Palestinian coast, and it had gained renown as a centre for quality textile production. The city occupied a unique geographical position: perched on an island in the middle of a lake (Lake Manzala today), it was watered on one side by the Nile and separated from the Mediterranean on the other side by a narrow sliver of land. This prime location, however, caused its eventual demise. In later centuries repeated attacks by Crusader fleets caused Tinnis to be evacuated and then finally abandoned in 1227, never to be resettled.

Much of Tinnis's rich history was lost after its destruction. Of the little that remains, a considerable portion comes from Ibn Bassam's history, the *Anis al-jalis fi-akhbar Tinnis* ('Companion's Guide to the History of Tinnis'). Writing in the genre of city histories that was becoming increasingly popular, Ibn Bassam brought Tinnis to life. Amongst the details, he describes the city's pleasant climate, provides measurements of the city itself and its Friday Mosque, and includes an intricate record of Tinnis's commercial life:

The city had exactly 50 merchant inns and covered markets. Then six large buildings for merchants were constructed in 405 (1014–1015), making the total of 56 ... The city has 2,500 shops and 100 presses, employing a varying number of workers, from a minimum of two to a maximum of 20. There are 150 shops that specialize in the sale of cloth and various garments. There are 160 mills, some with one grinding stone, some with two, and some with five stones for husking and kneading. There are 36 bathhouses, excluding the baths in the private residences ... The city has 5,000 weaving looms, employing 10,000 workers, not including the men and women who embroider or adorn clothes... The city produces cloth, the like of which is not to be seen elsewhere: woven gilded cloths that look as if they were sewn, selling for 1,000 dinars each; headdresses, selling at 500 dinars each, sofas, selling for 1,000 dinars each, canopies, robe-sized cloth, beds, curtains, velvet cloth, eye-figured cloth, *dabiqi* silken cloth embroidered with silver, *dabiqi* unicoloured cloth, tabby cloth, and other things which cannot be described.[3]

The suburbs of Tinnis are also described by Ibn Bassam, including the city's great *diwan*, where Fatimid government offices would have been located. He notes that 372 fishing vessels and ferries operated from the island, and he lists the wide range of fish and bird species found in

Tinnis's environs. He also describes the challenges of living in Tinnis – the necessity to regularly import grain and wheat due to a lack of farmland, and to harness fresh water by pumping it through a complex system of canals, waterwheels, and cisterns. When describing the people of Tinnis, Ibn Bassam takes on a nostalgic tone:

> The people of the city are full of joy and happiness. They listen to music, are always delightful, seek comfort and shun anything that causes toil and hardship. They are fond of painting, drawing, embroidery, and dyeing. They do not get irritated when travelling, are tactful with their companions and do their utmost for their friends, give generously to those who ask for their help, and are fond of foreigners and travellers.[4]

Tinnis's economy thrived on its linen products, and by Ibn Bassam's time the city had become particularly famous for its *tiraz*.

Flax, Linen, and Tiraz

The common flax plant is given the Latin name *usitatissimum* ('most useful') for its wide range of uses – as a food item, as a source of linseed oil, and especially for making linen. By the 10th century, Egypt had already long been an important centre of flax cultivation and linen production. Under the Fatimids, however, these industries became central to the country's flourishing economy and were fuelled especially by the production of *tiraz*.

Stemming from the Persian word for 'adorn-ment' or 'embellishment', the term '*tiraz*' has multiple usages but commonly refers to textiles containing bands of embroidered writing. These textiles could come in a range of styles, includ-ing robes, headdresses, or scarves, with the embroidered writing found on sleeves, hems, and collars.

Most significant was the *tiraz* upon which was embroidered the name of the Fatimid Imam-caliphs. The production of official *tiraz* was the sole prerogative of the Imam-caliphs, mirroring their exclusive privilege to be named on coins and in Friday sermons. Official textiles contained the Imam-caliph's name, a benediction, and the place of production, and they became highly sought after for their material as well as symbolic value. With many royal *tiraz* factories like those of Tinnis owned and controlled by the state, *tiraz* production became an important source of revenue for the Fatimid government.

While *tiraz* was also produced under other Muslim dynasties, it reached its high point in Fatimid Egypt. Wearing *tiraz* became central to the sartorial fashion of the Fatimid court, and when its style became sought after by the upper echelons of Egyptian society, the consequent high demand catalysed production across the country. The causes for this cultural phenomenon are manifold and include the influence of courtly culture on everyday life, but one likely critical factor was belief in the *baraka* (blessings) of the Imam-caliphs themselves.

Figure 19. Fatimid *Tiraz* Fragment

Tiraz textile fragment, approximately 4 ½ x 6 inches. This sumptuous linen and silk woven textile has been dated to the era of the Imam-caliph al-Hafiz (r. 1130–1149).

Sometime during the reign of al-Zahir, a special mark of honour was requested by a Fatimid official. Al-Musabbihi records that the official had sought:

a robe from among the robes of our *mawla* [al-Zahir], and a skullcap (*shashiyya*) . . . that he [al-Zahir] has worn.[5]

The request appealed to a long-standing practice. When Jawhar set out from Ifriqiya to Egypt, the Imam-caliph al-Muʿizz had seen him off in a formal farewell ceremony. Upon his return to his palace, al-Muʿizz:

removed all the garments he had been wearing, except his trousers and his signet ring and sent them to Jawhar.[6]

The practice of granting caliphal clothing (*khil'a*) constituted an important ritual in the ceremonials of earlier and contemporaneous Muslim imperial courts. With textiles retaining high value in medieval societies, such gifts bestowed both economic value and symbolic honour to the recipient. This was also true for the granting of preciously adorned *tiraz* containing the names of ruling caliphs. Under the Fatimids, such practices gained special significance. To their followers, the clothing and *tiraz* of the Imam-caliphs served as mediums of sanctity and blessing. This hearkened back to established precedents, notably those of the Prophet Muhammad's companions seeking his hair clippings, which was later reflected in the corpus of pious literature regarding blessings accrued from the Prophet's cloak (*burda*).

Today, Fatimid *tiraz* fabrics are housed across several museums and collections and form an important subject of ongoing research. Many were discovered during archaeological surveys of tombs and cemeteries, with others used by Christian Crusaders to wrap holy relics. Historians suggest that such *tiraz* embroidered with the Imam's name in funerary contexts were used as burial shrouds for the deceased. They were probably meant to invoke for the departed the intercession of the imam, and his forefather the Prophet Muhammad.

Connections to the Indian Ocean

By the 11th century, the Fatimid Empire stretched southwards along the Nile to Nubia (present-day southern Egypt and northern Sudan) and eastwards to the Red Sea. Its maritime influence radiated far further, however, extending to the shores of the Indian Ocean and beyond. Besides being lucrative avenues for trade, connections across the Indian Ocean provided vibrant conduits for the growth of the Ismaili *da'wa*, with Yemen serving as a vital hub.

Yemen had for centuries served as the crossroads between the heartlands of the Muslim world and the lands of the Indian Ocean. Long a bastion of the *da'wa*, it was from Yemen that the founding Ismaili *da'i*, Abu Abd Allah al-Shi'i had set out for Ifriqiya, and from Yemen that other *da'is* had traversed the seas to establish the Ismaili *da'wa* in Multan in the Indian subcontinent.

Maps of the Indus Valley and the Indian Ocean appear as notable features in the *Book of Curiosities*. There, they mark stops on the 'musk road' between India, Tibet, and China. The knowledge of such routes was perhaps gleaned from Ismaili *da'is* and the traders of Multan, and their appearance showcases the trade and cultural linkages between Cairo and the world of the Indian Ocean.

It was also from Yemen and the Red Sea that Fatimid commercial influence extended towards East Africa. In 1984, the discovery of the Mtambwe coin hoard near Pemba in Tanzania testified to the wide circulation of Fatimid coins. An established maritime route from Egypt to East Africa is also evident in the *Book of Curiosities*, with detailed depictions of the Horn of Africa, the Somalian coast, Zanzibar and beyond. Of the items traded between East Africa and Fatimid Egypt, it was probably rock crystal that received the most dazzling reception in Cairo, with that mined in Madagascar perhaps the source of some

Figure 20. Fatimid Coins
Examples of Fatimid gold and silver coins that would have been used across the trade networks, including along the Egypt and East African routes.

of the most famed Fatimid artefacts that survive today.

Fatimid Rock Crystal

Rock crystal (*billawr*) is a form of quartz or crystallized rock that is transparent yet extremely hard. It was famed in the medieval era, and it required skilled lapidaries to turn it into ornamentation. In Fatimid Egypt, the Imam-caliphs' patronage saw this expertise reach unrivalled heights, producing treasures that became highly sought after both in Muslim and Christian lands. For many, it is the material's unique relationship with light that gave it an enduring appeal:

Figure 21. Fatimid Rock Crystal Ewer (San Marco Basilica)

Inscribed on the neck of this rock crystal ewer is the name of Imam-caliph al-Aziz.

Why rock crystal? Because of its translucency, its multiple planes, and the fascination of its colours – all of which present themselves differently as light moves around them. The hues of rock crystal are subtle, striking and widely varied – for they can be clear or milky, white, or rose coloured, or smoky, or golden, or black.

It is because of these qualities that rock crystal seems to be such an appropriate symbol of the profound beauty and the ever-unfolding mystery of Creation itself – and the Creator.[7]

Surviving Fatimid rock crystal pieces are amongst the most valuable works of Islamic art today. The ewer in the treasury of San Marco in Venice is one such piece, crafted from a block of flawless rock crystal. On its surface is an inscription pronouncing the name of al-Aziz bi'llah. Another crescent-shaped rock crystal ornament housed today in the Germanisches Nationalmuseum, Nuremburg, Germany, may well have once been a pendant. The base is inscribed with praise for the Imam-caliph al-Zahir li-I'zaz Din Allah.

Chapter 7

The Fluctuations of Fatimid Rule

The 11th century saw both the pinnacle of the Fatimid Empire and the beginnings of its drawn-out eclipse. It encompassed al-Zahir's reign and the 58-year reign of Imam-caliph al-Mustansir bi'llah (1036–94) – the latter being the longest reign of any ruler in Islamic history. The century witnessed the pronouncement of Fatimid sovereignty in Abbasid Baghdad for almost a year, but it also witnessed the shrinking of the empire's borders, the ravages of famine and civil war, the rule of military overlords, and an irrevocable succession crisis. Yet, as the fortunes of the *dawla* vacillated, those of the *da'wa* thrived especially in Yemen and Iran.

Al-Musabbihi and the Yearning for Past Years
Al-Zahir was 18 years old when his aunt Sitt al-Mulk passed away. Her steadying hand may have been quickly missed, for factional politics soon returned, running rampant in the army and the court and precluding al-Zahir from the levers of power. The receding of the Nile in 1024 compounded the crisis, with drought and famine exacerbating civil unrest and sectarian strife.

For the *amir* Mukhtar al-Musabbihi, the return to factionalism may have invoked despondency. He was born in Egypt in 977 to an Arab family, was a devout Sunni, and had joined the Fatimid army before being promoted to governorships in Egypt and then embarking on a career in the *diwan*s. Al-Musabbihi lived through al-Hakim's and much of al-Zahir's reigns. A scholar and literary figure, al-Musabbihi composed poetry and wrote on wide-ranging topics, from astronomy to cooking to a history of those afflicted by love. Most famous, however, was his *Akhbar Misr*, a massive work relating Egypt's history up to his own lifetime. In this work, in diary-like fashion, al-Musabbihi wrote about major and mundane events, including unusual events like the sighting of a hippopotamus in the Nile. While much of the work has been lost, lengthy excerpts survive in later works. Aged 18 when al-Hakim began his reign, al-Musabbihi became a trusted figure to the Imam-caliph, and in his history, he related direct testimonies from al-Hakim, including that of the Imam-caliph's final moments with his father al-Aziz.

In the aftermath of al-Hakim's passing, al-Musabbihi continued to record events in the capital. These included the plots and power struggles between different parties at court that collectively resulted in the distancing of al-Zahir from power. When al-Musabbihi passed away in 1030 aged 53, a sense of yearning for previous decades likely lingered.

The New Regencies

The fractious struggles at the court eventually resulted in a victor, when in 1027 Ahmad al-Jarjaraʿi emerged as vizier. He was a migrant of Iraqi origin who had once served under the patronage of Sitt al-Mulk. The chroniclers relate that his hands had been amputated in al-Hakim's reign for peculation, but he nonetheless remained a key official and emerged as a major power broker in al-Zahir's reign. As vizier, al-Jarjaraʿi was able to restore a semblance of political order, aided by the fulsome rise of the Nile. Soon thereafter another natural calamity reared its head.

Pandemics are no strangers to human history, and outbreaks of the plague had long wreaked death and chaos in the Mediterranean basin. In 1036, a recurrence of the plague afflicted Egypt. The Imam-caliph al-Zahir, then 31 years old, succumbed to the illness, and passed away shortly thereafter.

Six years earlier, in 1030, amidst jubilant celebrations, a newborn son of al-Zahir had been publicly declared *wali al-ahd*. Named Maʿadd, after his great-grandfather Maʿadd al-Muʿizz li-Din Allah, he would become the eighth Fatimid Imam-caliph, with the regnal title *al-Mustansir bi'llah* (He Who Asks God for Aid). While announcing a successor at such a young age was seemingly exceptional, in those years of upheaval, famine, and plague, it may well be that al-Zahir foresaw the necessity of a clear and undisputed appointment.

Al-Mustansir bi'llah was seven years old at the time of his father's passing. Symbolizing where power then lay, it was the vizier al-Jarjara'i who placed the turban crown upon the young Imam's head at the enthronement in 1036. Over the next nine years, al-Jarjara'i operated as ruler in all but name, competently restoring Egypt's economy after the ravages of the previous decade. Yet the power struggles continued to fester, becoming acutely apparent in Syria where it led to the fall of the Fatimid general Anush Tegin.

The Rise and Fall of Anush Tegin

Like many Turkish slave-soldiers, Anush Tegin's origins lay in central Asia. Captured whilst young in Khuttalon in present-day Tajikistan, he was then sold into slavery and bought by a Fatimid military official in Syria. Subsequently, Anush Tegin asked to enter the service of al-Hakim, and when the request was granted, he was enrolled as a slave-soldier (*ghulam*) in the military barracks in Cairo. Upon graduating in 1015, he was freed. Noticed by al-Hakim, Anush Tegin's career then saw a stellar ascent. By 1023 he was serving as the Fatimid military commander in Palestine.

Syria and Palestine were then once more beset by turmoil, with Bedouin confederations agitating against Fatimid rule and seizing significant portions of the country, including Aleppo in 1024. When Anush Tegin was defeated by Bedouin forces, the politicking at the capital saw his recall to Egypt in 1026 and subsequent imprisonment at the hands of a hostile vizier. In 1029, however, with Fatimid fortunes in Syria reeling once again,

Anush Tegin's expertise was required. The new vizier al-Jarjara'i dispatched the Turkish general once more to the region to lead a Fatimid expedition. This time, on the banks of Lake Tiberias, Anush Tegin led the Fatimid army to a major victory against the Bedouin tribes and soon after entered Damascus to take his post as governor. Fatimid authority under Anush Tegin was restored across most of the country over the following years, with the general retaking Aleppo in 1038. For almost 60 years, Fatimid fortunes had waxed and waned in Syria, but Anush Tegin soon emerged as perhaps the country's most competent and popular Fatimid governor.

Yet Anush Tegin's accomplishments would also prove to be his downfall. Fearing his meteoric success and seeming independence, al-Jarjara'i and his cadre plotted the general's disgrace. The general would be cursed from the pulpits of Cairo as a rebel and his army made to abandon him. Doomed to spend his final days besieged in the citadel of Aleppo, he died in 1042. The long sought-after consolidation of Fatimid rule in Syria perished with him. In his final hours, Anush Tegin may well have felt his services remained unrecognized. However, in 1057 Imam-caliph al-Mustansir bi'llah ordered the exhumation of his body from Aleppo. As his coffin passed through Syria and Palestine, Fatimid military officers paid their respects, and he was ceremonially reinterred in Jerusalem.

In Cairo, the period of relative stability under al-Jarjara'i had come to an end when the vizier passed away in 1044. Thereafter, the endemic political struggles entered another phase with the rise to power of a new contingent led by al-Sayyida Rasad, the queen mother.

The Rise of al-Sayyida Rasad, the Queen Mother
Chroniclers report little about al-Sayyida Rasad's early life. A slave of Sudanese, Nubian, or Ethiopian origin, she had been brought to Egypt and by 1030 was a consort of the Imam-caliph al-Zahir. When in 1030 her eight-month-old son – the future Imam-caliph al-Mustansir bi'llah – was proclaimed heir apparent, Rasad's own stature rose as the future queen mother. In time, she developed a significant network of commercial interests and charitable endowments.

By the time of al-Jarjara'i's death, al-Sayyida Rasad had already emerged as a formidable force. Thereafter, Rasad's own network of representatives emerged in increasing rivalry with the factions of ministers already dominating the government *diwan*s, leading to occasionally violent conflict. In 1050, Rasad's ascendency was realized when she secured the appointment of one of her protégés, the Sunni Hanafi judge Abu Muhammad al-Yazuri (d. 1058), as the new vizier.

Rasad's regency saw a major development with the recruitment of Nubian and Sudanese slave-soldiers into the Fatimid army. While having precedence in previous administrations, it gathered pace under Rasad as thousands were brought, armed, and garrisoned in Cairo and across Egypt. Labelled in the sources as the 'purchased slaves' (*abid al-shira*), they became a powerful contingent, loyal to Rasad, and served as a counterforce to the long-established Berber and Turkish contingents.

Rasad wielded considerable power over the following years, leading the 13th-century Egyptian historian Ibn Muyassar to remark that it was Rasad who 'ruled' over the *dawla*.[1] Yet while medieval authors often adopted a censuring tone when reporting women's involvement in statecraft, in Rasad's case, there is perhaps a further underlying racial bias in the medieval reports about her, and the subsequent role of Africans in the Fatimid army.

Attitudes towards blackness by medieval Arabic writers fluctuated across time and place and had varying underlying conceptions when compared to the geneticized racialist classifications of the 19th and 20th centuries. They were nonetheless often conditioned by constructions of colour and social hierarchies in which blackness was seen as a disadvantage, or even a curse. Work on racism and attitudes towards colour in medieval Muslim societies has become an important avenue of historical research in recent years. A critical study of the presence of often hostile representations of Africans in medieval accounts of Fatimid history, including those concerning Rasad and her supporters – on whom blame for subsequent calamities was often pinned – remains to be undertaken.

From the onset of his reign, political machinations at the Fatimid court kept the Imam-caliph al-Mustansir from the corridors of power. Yet over the same period, the recognition of his religious authority would surge across the Muslim world through the flourishing of the Fatimid *da'wa*.

Al-Mu'ayyad fi'l-Din al-Shirazi

By the 11th century, the lush metropolis of Shiraz in south-western Iran was a well-established nucleus in the Fatimid *da'wa* network. There, in 1000, Hibat Allah Ahmad, known more commonly as *da'i* al-Mu'ayyad fi'l-Din al-Shirazi, was born into a family steeped in the *da'wa*. Amongst his important surviving works, al-Mu'ayyad's autobiography (*sira*) remains a critical source for historians of the 11th-century Fatimid world.

Al-Mu'ayyad was the son of the chief Fatimid *da'i* of Fars, and by his 30s he had begun leading the Ismaili community of Shiraz. The city was then ruled by the Buyid *amir* Abu Kalijar (d. 1048), and it had a majority Sunni populace with significant Shi'i communities residing in the city and its vicinity. Abu Kalijar's army reflected this diversity, with his Turkish soldiery belonging to the Sunni traditions and his Daylami contingents increasingly adhering to the Fatimid *da'wa*. In his *sira*, al-Mu'ayyad recalls how his house served as a meeting place for the community and that on Tuesdays the Daylami soldiers would attend *majalis* delivered by al-Mu'ayyad himself.

The growth of the Fatimid *da'wa*, however, saw the heightening of rivalries in Shiraz. Fearing conflict within his own army and seeking resolution, the Buyid ruler held public disputations (*munazaras*) between al-Mu'ayyad and local Sunni *qadi*s. These debates revolved around the necessity of the interpretation of the Qur'an and its inner meanings (*ta'wil*). Al-Mu'ayyad's rendition of the debates reiterate the centrality of the Fatimid doctrine of the imamate. Upholding Qur'anic injunctions and prophetic precedents that the Qur'an requires *ta'wil*, al-Mu'ayyad asserts that the only authoritative guides to the meaning of scripture are those charged with authority (*ulu'l-amr*), as declared in Q. 4:83. These guides are the Imams from the *ahl al-bayt*, in whom authoritative knowledge of the inner realities of the Qur'an is divinely vested. Al-Mu'ayyad's rivals, however, gained the upper hand, compelling the *da'i* to leave his home city.

Around 1045, the *da'i* al-Mu'ayyad arrived in Cairo. Despite his eminence in the *da'wa*, al-Mu'ayyad was denied an audience with the Imam-caliph al-Mustansir for two years – a testament to the power of the court elite who probably mistrusted this outsider. On 18 February 1048, he was finally granted permission to see the Imam-caliph.

My eyes had barely fallen on him [the Imam-caliph] when awe took hold of me and reverence overcame me; and it appeared to me as though I was standing in front of the Messenger of God and the Commander of the Faithful Ali, may God's blessings be upon

them, and (that I was) facing their counten-
ances . . . I increased in tongue-tiedness and
in storming up the steep hill of stammering,
and he – may God perpetuate his kingdom –
kept saying, 'Let him be until he calms down
and becomes accustomed.'

Then I arose, took his noble hand, and
kissed it and placed it upon my eyes and
breast, and bade farewell and left.[2]

Four years later, al-Mu'ayyad secured a position in the government chancery, where his
career as diplomat and negotiator would come
to the fore.

Combatting the Seljuks in Baghdad

The arrival of the Seljuk Turks from Central Asia
into Iran and Iraq signalled a major transformation in the 11th-century Muslim world. Centred
initially in eastern Iran, by 1055 the Seljuk
dynasty had wrested Baghdad away from the
Buyids. As the leaders of their Turkish tribal
confederation, the Seljuk rulers also presented
themselves as defenders of Sunni Islam and
protectors of the Abbasid caliphs. With their
continued march westwards, conflict with the
Fatimids in Syria became inevitable.

The *da'i* al-Mu'ayyad emerged as a principal
protagonist in the defence of the Fatimid Empire's
western borders. Operating under the vizierate of
al-Yazuri, from 1056 to 1057, he secured a coalition of local Syrian and Iraqi *amir*s, Bedouin
chiefs, and Turkish generals to halt the Seljuk

advance. To spearhead the alliance, al-Mu'ayyad travelled to Syria to bring Arslan al-Basasiri (d. 1060) into the coalition. Al-Basasiri, a prominent Turkish general who commanded significant forces in Iraq, soon won a decisive victory over the Seljuks in northern Iraq. As had been the case in al-Hakim's reign, the name of the Fatimid Imam-caliph was soon after pronounced in Mosul.

Two years later, al-Mu'ayyad and his allies achieved what became a major milestone in Fatimid history. On 1 January 1059, al-Basasiri secured control of Baghdad. For 40 consecutive weeks, the Imam-caliph al-Mustansir bi'llah's name was invoked in the congregational mosques of the Abbasid capital. Seljuk forces, however, remained formidable. After a counterattack, they reinstated Abbasid authority in the city in 1060. They then turned to Syria, which would irreversibly fall out of the Fatimid orbit.

The Da'i *of* Da'is

Al-Mu'ayyad's career reached its apogee in 1060 when he was appointed chief *da'i* by al-Mustansir bi'llah. In time, his teachings – in both prose and poetry – became seminal articulations of the Ismaili faith; the texts of many of his *majalis* sessions are published today under the title *al-Majalis al-Mu'ayyadiya.*[3] The *da'i* then also spearheaded efforts to protect and transfer the vast corpus of Fatimid Ismaili literature. In 1062, al-Mu'ayyad oversaw the sending of major Fatimid texts to Yemen in the care of a prominent Yemeni *da'i* who had come to Cairo. Continuously reproduced over the following centuries, much of this corpus was later transferred by the Tayyibi *da'wa* to India, where the texts continue to be preserved and studied, and from where they entered into academic scholarship in the 20th century.

In 1078, al-Mu'ayyad passed away. He was laid to rest in Cairo's *Dar al-Ilm* (House of Knowledge) in tribute to his learning and acumen. His legacy lived on not only through his works and accomplishments, but also through his mentoring of some of the most influential *da'i*s of the next generation, including Nasir-i Khusraw.

Hakim Nasir-i Khusraw

The *da'i* Nasir-i Khusraw stands today as a key figure in the Central Asian Ismaili tradition and as an esteemed luminary of Iranian cultural and literary history.

Born around 1004 in Qubadiyan in present-day Tajikistan, Nasir-i Khusraw was raised by a family of landowners and officials. Schooled in Arabic and Persian, he gained expertise in the religious and natural sciences, and grew up at a time when the region was undergoing a renaissance of Persian language and culture. By the time he was in his 30s he had an established career in the Ghaznavid and Seljuk administrations. When later writing about the milestones that promoted his deep-rooted spiritual transformation, Nasir spoke of a dream that he had in 1045 when he was aged around 42. There, as

Figure 22. Opening Page of *al-Majalis al-Mu'ayyadiya*

The *Majalis al-Mu'ayyadiya* is a collection of lectures on Ismaili doctrine delivered by the chief *da'i* al-Mu'ayyad to initiates. These lectures would have been pre-approved by the Imam-caliph.

Nasir relays, a voice admonished him for pursu-
ing the pleasures of life, and pointing to Mecca,
the figure in his dream commanded him to seek
wisdom:

> When I awoke, I remembered everything,
> which had truly made a great impression on
> me. 'You have waked from last night's sleep,'
> I said to myself. 'When are you going to wake
> from that of forty years?' And I reflected that
> until I changed all my ways, I would never
> find happiness.[4]

After resigning from his post, Nasir set out on
a journey towards Mecca. In the years that
followed, he travelled from his hometown to Iran,
Azerbaijan, Armenia, Syria, Palestine, and finally
to Mecca and Medina as a pilgrim. An astute
observer of the human experience, he wrote
lucidly about what he saw and the people he met,
composing what was to become one of the famous
travelogues of the age. Nasir's *Safarnama* ('Book
of Travels') remains a key source for modern
historians on life in the medieval Muslim world.

Through the course of his life, Nasir pondered
questions pertaining to his faith: Were the Prophet
Muhammad's companions the most fortunate
of people because they had been able, under the
blessed tree, to place their hands in the Prophet's
own to give him their allegiance (alluding to
Q. 48:10)? In whose hands could he place his
own to take the oath, just as Muhammad's
companions had done? From whom could he

now, five centuries later, hear the true knowledge
of the revelation?

On 3 August 1047, Nasir arrived in Fatimid
Cairo, where he fulfilled his long-held quest:

> One day I reached a town before whose
>   greatness
> The heavens and the horizons seemed like
>   servants,
> Whose gardens were full of fruits and of
>   roses,
> Land full of trees and walls well
>   decorated . . .
> A town where my intelligence announced:
> This is the place to ask—don't go
>   away![5]

In Cairo, Nasir took the pledge of allegiance to
the Imam-caliph al-Mustansir, with whom he
was able to secure an audience in his three years
there. An ardent believer, Nasir studied under
the *da'i* al-Mu'ayyad, whom he credited as
another source of his transformation: 'Drop by
drop and day by day he fed me the healing potion
. . . I who had been as stone was now a ruby.'[6]
The itinerant traveller became a stalwart of the
da'wa, declaring in one of his poems: 'I am a
Fatimid, I am a Fatimid, I am a Fatimid.'[7]

Decades later, Nasir wrote about Cairo for his
Persian-speaking readership, recounting the
wealth of the city, the splendour of its mosques,
streets, bathhouses, and palaces. In one passage,
he describes the city's resplendent greenery:

If anyone wants to make a garden in Egypt it can be done during any season at all, since any tree, fruit-bearing or otherwise, can be obtained and planted. There are special people called *dallal*s who can obtain immediately any kind of fruit you desire, because they have trees planted in tubs on rooftops. Many roofs are gardens and most of what is grown is fruit-producing, such as oranges, pomegranates, apples, quinces, roses, herbs, and vegetables.[8]

In 1050, Nasir headed once more as a pilgrim to Mecca. Seven years later, he returned to Khurasan, now as the chief *da'i* of the region, having been awarded the most senior title of *hujja* (proof) by Imam-caliph al-Mustansir. Initially, Nasir's preaching gained success, until in 1064 heightened Seljuk hostility compelled him to migrate to Yumgan in today's north-western Afghanistan. There, an Ismaili *amir* called Ali b. Asad granted him protection.

In his final years, Nasir composed a prodigious corpus of scholarship and poetry, much of which survives today. A recurring theme in his oeuvre was the emphasis that God's greatest gift to humanity was the use of intellect.

Nasir also composed over 15,000 lines of poetry, his mastery of language rendering him one of the Persian-speaking world's most renowned poets whose verses still attract admirers today. The final years of Nasir-i Khusraw's life remain obscure, with his death surmised to be sometime after 1070. Today, in the Badakhshan region that now covers parts of Tajikistan, Afghanistan, eastern China, and Gilgit-Baltistan province of northern Pakistan, Nizari-Ismaili communities continue to revere the *da'i* as *pir* (guide) and as *Hakim Nasir* (the Wise Nasir).

Egypt's Great Calamity

The age of prosperity presented in the *Safarnama*'s depiction of Cairo came to a shuddering halt by the 1060s. In the two decades following his succession, the Imam-caliph al-Mustansir witnessed an array of ministers and family members seize power in his stead. In 1058, the vizier al-Yazuri was executed on charges of treason and corruption, his fall followed by a series of further factional struggles. These paved the way for the most devastating crisis to afflict the Fatimid Empire thus far. The years between 1062 and 1073 would generally be called 'The Great Calamity' (*al-shidda al-uzma*). This was a period of civil war, anarchy, and famine that resulted in death and starvation, refugee migrations, and a permanent alteration in the country's political landscape.

The *shidda* was sparked by the spread of factional fighting to the military, when Turkish and Berber contingents of the Fatimid army turned against the new Nubian battalions. Outside the walls of Cairo in 1062, a battle between the two sides resulted in a victory for the Turkish–Berber faction, led by their general Nasir al-Dawla b. Hamdan, a descendant of Syria's Hamdanid dynasty who himself had risen in the Fatimid ranks. Though defeated, the Nubians were not decimated, and many moved northwards to the Nile delta. Warfare between the different contingents continued for much of the next five years. Across Egypt and in the delta especially, marauding factions from different sides destroyed farmlands, lawlessness became rampant, and agriculture ground to a halt.

Between 1067 and 1072, a devastating famine gripped Egypt. As its grain stores became depleted and starvation led to loss of life, many who could escape – including members of the Imam-caliph's own family – sought refuge in other countries. It would take Egypt decades to recover from the depopulation.

Between 1068 and 1069, then aged nearly 40, the Imam-caliph al-Mustansir himself took to the battlefield to restore order. Leading battalions that included Turks who now opposed the powerful Nasir al-Dawla, al-Mustansir won a victory that forced the general to retreat northwards. The respite proved transient. Reinforced by Bedouins and Berber tribesmen, Nasir al-Dawla soon regained control of Cairo. There, in vengeance, and reportedly hoping to pronounce the authority of the Abbasids as rulers, Nasir al-Dawla kept al-Mustansir confined to the palace on a meagre pension.

During the years of conflagrations and anarchy, the treasury was bare, and ministers and soldiers took to looting the Fatimid palaces and libraries in 1067/1068 as recompense for payment. Medieval chroniclers relate how treasures and precious manuscripts were hauled away on pack animals, never to be returned. But in those darkest of days, it was Fustat that suffered the brunt of the anarchy, as whole quarters of once bustling streets were razed to the ground.

In 1073, Nasir al-Dawla and his family were murdered by rivals from amongst the Turkish contingents. It was then that the Imam-caliph al-Mustansir wrote to Badr al-Jamali, the Fatimid governor of Acre, to come and stem the depravation.

The Rise of Badr al-Jamali

Badr al-Jamali was born around 1015, a slave of Armenian origins. Recruited into the Fatimid army, he ascended through the ranks and twice gained the governorship of Damascus before attaining command of Acre on the Mediterranean coast. His power was bolstered by the support of his own Armenian bodyguard and loyal troops. The invitation from the Imam-caliph reached Badr in the winter of 1073, a time when travel by sea was especially dangerous. Nevertheless, intrepidly, he readied 100 ships to sail the Mediterranean, and soon alighted on Egypt's shores.

The arrival of Badr took many of Egypt's factional leaders by surprise. Rapid military engagements saw Badr quickly emerge as the unrivalled power over the country. With the famine also having ended and tax revenues once more refilling state coffers, the *shidda* came to an end.

The nature of the Fatimid Empire would now for ever after change with the beginning of a new era of military rule. For the next 20 years (1074–94), Badr al-Jamali ruled as the supreme military commander of Egypt. With his rule legitimized by al-Mustansir's sovereignty, the general often styled himself 'Badr al-Mustansiri' to signify his position as a servant of the Imam-caliph, and relations between Badr and al-Mustansir generally remained cordial. Nonetheless, Badr's rise precluded al-Mustansir from power. Backed by his personal guard, called the *juyushiyya*, Badr assumed all the major offices of the state, including that of vizier and chief justice. In 1077, after the passing of the *da'i* al-Mu'ayyad, Badr styled himself as the chief *da'i*. But of all the titles acquired by him, most significant was that of *amir al-juyush* (commander of the armies), which affirmed the inexorable shift in Fatimid governance.

From Empire to Egyptian State

The decades of factionalism, the civil war, and the ravages of the *shidda* had taken their toll on the Fatimid Empire. By 1073, its borders had shrunk considerably, and the empire was reduced to an almost exclusively Egyptian state, with a critical presence on the Syrian coast.

In North Africa, the sovereignty of the Fatimids had ended when the Zirid dynasty of governors succumbed to the dominance of the Maliki Sunni *ulama*. As early as 1016/1017, anti-Ismaili mobs impelled by segments of the Maliki *ulama* had launched bloody massacres against the followers of the Fatimid *da'wa* in

Qayrawan, Tunis, Tripoli, and even al-Mahdiyya. In 1048/1049, the Zirid viceroys recognized the authority of the Abbasids, and thus pronounced their own independence from the Fatimids.

In Syria, the fortunes of the Fatimids had also waned. In 1070, Arab *amir*s of the Mirdasid dynasty who had once supported the Fatimids succumbed to Seljuk pressure and pronounced the authority of the Abbasids instead. With much of the northern Syrian populace then belonging to the various Shiʿi communities – including Ismailis, Ithnaʿasharis, and Nusyaris – this was met with popular opposition, but Aleppo nonetheless fell out of Fatimid control. By 1078, Damascus also had come under direct Seljuk rule.

Seljuk ascendance also swept away Fatimid control over Mecca and Medina. In 1070 the *ashraf* of Mecca transferred their allegiance to the Abbasids, ending almost a century of Fatimid allegiance. Fatimid suzerainty over Mecca and Medina was briefly restored in al-Mustansir's name from 1074 to 1081, but it ceased thereafter.

The two-decade rule of Badr al-Jamali nonetheless saw an important recasting of the Fatimid presence in Egypt. With stability restored, the city of Cairo thrived as a cosmopolitan centre. To symbolize this new era, Badr al-Jamali built a new fortified wall around the city in the 1080s. Made of stone with a limestone facing to beautify the exterior, the wall's aesthetics elicited much admiration. Imposing gateways were also built above the city's main entrances. These gateways survive to this day as remarkable examples of Fatimid architecture.

Badr's presence also catalysed new waves of migration, with many Armenian soldiers and families coming to settle in Egypt. While some joined the *juyushiyya* as soldiers, others plied their trade as craftsmen and tradesmen; newly arrived Christian priests brought their unique litanies and their churches. They added to the diversity of life in the capital.

In 1094, Badr al-Jamali passed away, aged over 80. By then, the general had entrenched his family in positions of power, having promoted his sons through the ranks of the army and married one of his daughters, Sitt al-Mulk, to Abu'l-Qasim Ahmad, the youngest son of the Imam-caliph al-Mustansir.

With Badr's demise, his son Abu'l-Qasim Shahanshah, commonly known by his title al-Afdal, took the reins. Then aged 28, and supported by the *juyushiyya*, al-Afdal was able to enforce his appointment as vizier by al-Mustansir, and as the new *amir al-juyush*, he soon emerged as the kingmaker in the Fatimid realms.

The Question of Succession

In December 1094, after a reign spanning nearly six decades, the Imam-caliph al-Mustansir bi'llah passed away. For the first time in Fatimid history, the succession process resulted in civil war. While rival claims to authority between family members was common in most medieval dynasties, as the authority of the Fatimid

sovereign was divinely decreed according to
Fatimid Ismaili doctrine, the process of succession necessarily took on religious salience.

The central question was which of
al-Mustansir's sons had been appointed as
successor to the imamate: Nizar, his eldest, or
Ahmad, his youngest. The contesting claims
would split the Fatimid *da'wa*, culminating in
the emergence of two distinct communities,
followed in time by a third. The Nizari and
Tayyibi traditions, which form the two principal
Ismaili communities in the world today, share a
common heritage in their allegiance to the line
of Imams to the Imam-caliph al-Mustansir
bi'llah. Thereafter, they part on the question of
his successor, tracing the continuity of the
imamate in either Nizar or Ahmad al-Musta'li
respectively.

Al-Mustafa li-Din Allah and al-Musta'li bi'llah

In September 1045, al-Mustansir had celebrated
the birth of Nizar, his eldest son. Little biographical information survives about Nizar's early
years, the extant material focussing mainly on
events that followed al-Mustansir's passing, when
Nizar was almost 50 years old. The prince had
grown up witnessing the vicissitudes of the
shidda, and in his adult years he was appointed
by the Imam-caliph as his successor. Thereafter, a
loyal following coalesced around the new heir
apparent.

However, the years that followed coincided
with the ascent of Badr al-Jamali and his

household, and the sources report growing hostilities between the prince and the new cadre of generals. One chronicler relates how Nizar decried al-Afdal b. Badr al-Jamali's conduct after seeing the general riding in the Imam-caliph's palace when the custom was to walk as a sign of respect to the Imam. Others allege that when al-Mustansir instructed the army's commanders to pledge the oath of allegiance to Nizar, they were stopped from doing so by al-Afdal.

With al-Mustansir's passing, Nizar and his supporters expected his appointment as Imam-caliph. It was then, however, that the *amir al-juyush* al-Afdal took charge. The following day, in the throne room of the palace, Abu'l-Qasim Ahmad was proclaimed instead as the new Imam-caliph with the regnal title *al-Musta'li bi'llah* (the Elevated by God).

Born in 1074 and aged 20 at the time of his inauguration, al-Musta'li was the youngest son of al-Mustansir. Married to al-Afdal's sister, al-Musta'li benefitted from the protection of his brother-in-law al-Afdal, who stood as the bulwark against challenges to al-Musta'li's authority. Within a few decades, al-Musta'li's followers provided official accounts to delineate the legitimacy of his succession. These pronounced that al-Mustansir, in his final moments, had bestowed the *nass* on al-Musta'li, having always held special affection for his youngest son. Accordingly, any earlier indications of Nizar's succession were limited and had been ultimately revoked. For Nizar's supporters, however, the pronouncement of the *nass* was final, with the irrevocability of the *nass* a central tenet of Shiʻi Ismaili doctrine.

Whilst the specific sequence of events that followed the death of al-Mustansir is unclear in the sources, what is certain is that conflict quickly erupted. After al-Mustaʻli's proclamation as Imam-caliph, Nizar and his brother Abd Allah, accompanied by their supporters, hurriedly left the capital. In January 1095, Nizar arrived at Alexandria, where support for his succession had already galvanized. The city's governor, the Turkish general Nasir al-Dawla Alp Tegin, had previously been in Badr al-Jamali's service but at this critical juncture stood by Nizar. The chief *qadi* of the city, Jalal al-Dawla b. Ammar delivered an impassioned speech proclaiming Nizar as the rightful Imam-caliph, with the regnal title *al-Mustafa li-Din Allah* (the Chosen One of the Religion of God), and censured al-Afdal for displacing the line of the imamate. Befitting the prerogatives of the Imam-caliph, gold coins were minted in Nizar's name, one of which still survives today.[9]

With the proclamation of al-Mustafa li-Din Allah in Alexandria and al-Mustaʻli bi'llah in Cairo, two Fatimid Imam-caliphs now reigned concurrently in two different Egyptian cities for the best part of the year. Expectedly, warfare followed. The *amir al-juyush* al-Afdal marched to Alexandria but was defeated by the armed forces supporting Nizar, who had been bolstered by local support. In a world of changing loyalties, however, the winds soon turned in al-Afdal's favour. By the end of 1095, al-Afdal had regained his military superiority and returned to conquer Alexandria.

In the aftermath, Nizar, his brothers, and the *qadi* Ibn Ammar were taken prisoner to Cairo, where al-Afdal probably ordered their execution. Sources suggest retribution by then also extended across the city, with some Cairenes executed for having pronounced curses in the markets against al-Afdal's conduct. Many of al-Mustansir's remaining sons fled the capital, as well as some of Nizar's own children, with a number making their way to North Africa. The followers of Nizar – that is, the Nizari Ismailis – maintain that one of Nizar's sons escaped to the Caspian region in Iran, and in him the line of the imamate continued. There, a new Ismaili state established its base and would soon become the bastion of the Nizari *da'wa*.

Meanwhile, in Egypt, until the end of Fatimid rule there, the Musta'lian line of Imam-caliphs continued to reign. They were to suffer a further crisis of succession, however, within a generation.

The Flourishes of the Fatimid *Da'wa*

Despite the *shidda* and the succession crises of 1094 to 1095, in the latter decades of the century the Fatimid *da'wa* had achieved seminal milestones in the Muslim world. In Yemen and Iran, the *da'wa* had established roots that led to the genesis of two Ismaili states where the Fatimid legacy would long continue.

The Sulayhid Dynasty of Yemen

A country that had been steeped in the history of the Ismaili *da'wa*, Yemen saw the creation of a dynastic state led by a new generation of Fatimid Ismaili *da'is* by the 11th century. During that time, Yemen also witnessed the reign of a remarkable woman of the Fatimid period.

Key to this period of Yemen's history was Ali b. Muhammad al-Sulayhi. He was born in the mountainous Haraz region of Yemen, into the family of a Shafi'i Sunni *qadi*. He grew up in the early decades of the 11th century and became proficient in the religious sciences. His entry into the Fatimid *da'wa* under the discipleship of Yemen's chief *da'i* Sulayman al-Zawahi marked the beginnings of his stellar ascent.

Several dynastic powers were then contesting for control over Yemen, including those of the country's Shi'i Zaydi Imams and the Sunni Najahids. In 1047, having critically secured support from several prominent tribes, Ali al-Sulayhi publicly proclaimed the Fatimid *da'wa* in Yemen, with the approval of the Imam-caliph al-Mustansir. Sixteen years of warfare between Yemen's competing forces ensued. By 1063, however, Ali had secured Yemen's capital Sana'a and much of southern Yemen. When inaugurating his reign, Ali promised the Yemenis the right to maintain their own legal school, reminiscent of the famous *aman* of al-Mu'izz. A year later, an official decree from the Imam-caliph al-Mustansir appointed Ali's son, al-Mukarram Ahmad, as his successor. Al-Mukarram went on to marry the lady who would become immortalized in Yemeni history.

Arwa bt. Ahmad b. al-Sulayhi was born in 1048. She was eulogized by Yemeni historians for her erudition: her knowledge of the Qur'an, her excellence in glossing and interpreting texts, and her prodigious memorization of literary and historical writings. Arwa was aged 18 when she married her cousin, al-Mukarram Ahmad, the heir to Sulayhid rule. Celebrations quickly dissipated, however, when in 1066 the *da'i* Ali al-Sulayhi was assassinated by his Najahid rivals, and Sulayhid territorial control collapsed. Arwa's husband al-Mukarram Ahmad spent nearly two decades at war regaining almost all the previously lost Sulayhid domains.

Throughout al-Mukarram's long campaign, Arwa al-Sulayhi stayed in the Sulayhid capital of Dhu Jibla and administered the state and the *da'wa* on behalf of her husband. Her role took on permanence, however, when al-Mukarram was left partially paralysed by illness. When al-Mukarram passed away in 1084, Arwa soon after became the leader of the Sulayhids and head of the Fatimid *da'wa* in Yemen.

In a world shaped by medieval patriarchies, Arwa's rise to power was initially challenged by external powers and internal rivals. From Cairo, the Imam-caliph al-Mustansir bi'llah intervened by issuing a famous *sijill* which decreed that al-Mukarram al-Asghar, the son of Arwa and al-Mukarram Ahmad, was the successor to the Sulayhid state. Exceptionally, however, the

Imam-caliph also appointed Arwa as the regent as well as the *hujja* – the highest rank in the *da'wa* – placing Yemen, Sindh, and Gujarat in India under her authority. In 1097/1098, following the Nizari–Musta'li split, Arwa pronounced her allegiance to al-Musta'li bi'llah. Thereafter, she continued as regent, reigning for over 50 years, until 1137.

Evidently, many of Arwa's challenges as ruler were aggravated by her being a woman. The way her prominent stature was later rationalized by some medieval Yemeni scholars testifies to a perceived paradox for medieval historians. Building on prevailing notions of body and soul, some scholars then held that the human body was an 'envelope' serving as the receptacle for the soul, and it was the soul's deeds that rendered one 'male' or 'female'. Accordingly, because 'male' was superior to 'female', souls which perfected their knowledge and deeds became 'male' regardless of their physical sex. Thus, for such scholars, Queen Arwa was in fact 'a man'. Arwa's achievements nonetheless remain a beacon of pride for Yemenis, who affectionately call her 'the little Queen of Sheba'.

The Genesis of the Nizari State in Iran
The flourishing of the Fatimid *da'wa* in Yemen was soon followed by a similar flourishing in Iran. There, by 1094, the foundations of a new state of the *da'wa* were established by the intrepid *da'i* and statesman, Hasan-i Sabbah, one of the most famous *da'i*s of the age.

Hasan-i Sabbah was born in the northern Iranian city of Qom in the 1050s to an Ithna'ashari family, but he moved to the ancient city of Rayy where, aged 17, he joined the Ismaili *da'wa*. In 1072, he was directed by the leading *da'i* in the region to travel to the Fatimid court.

In the Cairo that Hasan encountered, the ravages of the *shidda* would probably still have been palpable, as would have been Badr al-Jamali's grip. For three years, Hasan stayed at the Fatimid capital, during which his relations with Badr deteriorated. Hostility between the *da'i* and the *amir al-juyush* soon escalated, probably abetted by Hasan's support for the heir apparent, Nizar b. al-Mustansir. First distanced from Cairo and then banished from Egypt entirely, Hasan set off towards North Africa, before going to Isfahan in June 1081. Hasan's experience in Egypt may well have convinced him that the *da'wa* required an alternative base.

Isfahan was then witnessing the heyday of the Seljuk Empire. It was the age of the 'Sunni revival', which had found renewed vigour after being championed by the Seljuk vizier Nizam al-Mulk (d. 1092). Into this shifting landscape Hasan-i Sabbah returned. As instructed by the Imam-caliph al-Mustansir, the *da'i* spent the next nine years travelling across Iran, gauging rising resentment against the Seljuks. Many Daylamis in the Caspian region had a long-standing affinity to Shi'i Islam, and by 1087 they responded to the Ismaili call.

Hasan's procurement of the fortress of Alamut (the Eagle's Nest) in 1090 proved to be a major milestone. Perched atop the Rudbar mountains in northern Iran, Alamut benefitted from remarkable natural defences, and became the bastion of a new Ismaili state in Iran. Soon, other *da'i*s under Hasan's command gained successes, notably in Quhistan in eastern Iran, where numerous towns and fortresses joined the *da'wa*. As expected, the Seljuk reaction was forceful, and by 1092 campaigns against Alamut and Quhistan were already underway. When the deaths of the vizier Nizam al-Mulk and the Seljuk sultan Malik Shah followed in quick succession, the Seljuk Empire itself descended into civil war, allowing the *da'wa* to continue its spread.

While Badr al-Jamali was the chief *da'i* in Fatimid Cairo, the *da'wa* in Iran pursued a largely independent course under Hasan-i Sabbah's leadership. In 1095, following the succession crisis in Egypt, Hasan and the Iranian *da'wa* proclaimed their allegiance to Nizar b. al-Mustansir. Following Nizar's death, they recognized the imamate of Nizar's son and successor, whose identity was kept concealed, but in whose name the Nizari *da'wa* continued, with Hasan occupying the highest organizational rank in the Nizari *da'wa* as *hujja* (proof) of the concealed Imam. Although the Nizari and Musta'lian *da'wa* henceforth severed ties, their fates would remain closely bound in the decades to come.

Chapter 8

Late Fatimid Egypt and the Heirs of Empire

While Fatimid Egypt emerged politically transformed in the late 11th century, the start of the
12th century looked set to continue the trend, as it
brought a new spate of challenges, often at the
hands of external powers such as the Crusaders
and the Seljuks. Yet in the new era of military rule,
Fatimid Egypt would see flourishes of prosperity,
especially in the patronage of religious rituals and
architecture. Fatimid rule was to continue until
internal crises and external invasions led to its
cessation in 1171.

The Fatimids and the Onset of the Crusades

In October 1097, armies originating in present-day
France, Italy, Germany, and England descended
upon the eastern Mediterranean coastline and
headed towards Antioch. In a campaign instigated
by the Pope of Rome, the armies sought to fulfil
a sacred vow: to stand as pilgrims at the Church
of the Holy Sepulchre in Jerusalem, the attested
site of Christ's resurrection. With crosses sewn on
their clothing symbolizing their 'crusade', the
struggle that earmarked Christian and Muslim
history for the better part of two centuries had
begun.

The Fatimid possessions in Syria and Palestine were the principal targets of the Crusade. Having taken Seljuk Antioch between 1097 and 1098, Crusader armies next set their sights on Fatimid Jerusalem, where they arrived in June 1099. Inside the holy city, both Jews and Muslims rallied to join the Fatimid garrison in defence. It proved futile. On 14 July, the Crusaders entered Jerusalem and an infamous bloodbath followed. Written by an anonymous Crusader soldier, the *Gesta Francorum* ('Deeds of the Franks') recounts how after the city's fall, the killings reached the Temple Mount, its holiest site, upon which stood the mosque of al-Aqsa and the Dome of the Rock:

> Our men followed, killing and slaying even to the Temple of Solomon, where the slaughter was so great that our men waded in blood up to their ankles.[1]

Over 10,000 people were killed. The Jews who had gathered in their synagogues for safety were not spared; their buildings were set alight. As the *Gesta Francorum* reports, the stench of death filled the streets:

> No one ever saw or heard of such slaughter of pagan people, for funeral pyres were formed from them like pyramids, and no one knows their number except God alone.[2]

The fall of Jerusalem sent shock waves across the Muslim world. From Fatimid Cairo, the reaction saw a Fatimid army head towards Jerusalem, led by the *amir al-juyush* al-Afdal. Near the Fatimid port-city of Ascalon – close to the Egyptian border – the Crusaders inflicted a crushing defeat, however, forcing al-Afdal's retreat. Yet the city of Ascalon itself held fast, serving as Fatimid Egypt's last bastion of defence. The Battle of Ascalon in 1099 marks for historians the end of the First Crusade. The Crusaders' resounding victories had given rise to new states on the Mediterranean coast: the Latin Kingdom of Jerusalem (the foremost of four new Crusader states), and the others centred at Tripoli, Antioch, and Edessa, each led by a different prince. Henceforth, the Fatimid future would be significantly shaped by the Crusader presence.

The Egyptian Revival
Having begun his reign aged 20, the Imam-caliph al-Musta'li reigned for only six years. While military power was held by his brother-in-law al-Afdal, al-Musta'li expended considerable effort in bolstering the cause of the Musta'lian *da'wa*, especially in supporting the Sulayhids of Yemen. In 1101, aged 26, he passed away from natural causes.

Five years earlier in 1096, the Fatimid household had celebrated the birth of al-Musta'li's son, al-Mansur. Aged five upon his father's death, he was proclaimed the new Imam-caliph with the title *al-Amir bi-Ahkam Allah* (the One Who Commands by the Rulings of God).

The accession of al-Amir at such a young age solidified the rule of the *amir al-juyush* al-Afdal, which extended for two more decades. A large part of those years saw al-Afdal embroiled in warfare as he sought to stem the Crusader advance. From 1102 to 1111, the Fatimid Syrian cities of Tartus, Acre, Tripoli, and Sidon fell to Crusader forces, causing waves of refugees to flee to Egypt and other neighbouring countries. In 1117, the Crusader threat extended to Egypt itself when the king of Jerusalem, Baldwin I, invaded the country, capturing Farama and reaching Tinnis. The attack was only reversed when Baldwin passed away en route.

Despite the Crusader advance, al-Afdal's rule saw a return of heightened prosperity to the country. Major reforms were enacted, continuing some initiated by al-Afdal's father Badr al-Jamali, including those relating to coinage and the correlation of lunar and solar calendars. Especially important was the reorganization of Egypt's provincial boundaries, to facilitate the move towards tax-farming (*iqta*) systems which were then increasingly dominating the Muslim world.

By 1121, al-Afdal had ruled as vizier for 27 years. Though the Fatimids had ceded their Syrian possessions to the Crusaders by this time, Egypt had experienced a return to prosperity. But as repeated assassination attempts demonstrated, there were several opponents to al-Afdal's rule. By this time, the Imam-caliph al-Amir had reached adulthood. The rule of al-Afdal had, however, seen al-Amir largely kept away from power. In that year, as Ibn Khallikan relates:

> As al-Afdal rode forth from his house at
> the Imperial palace, he was attacked by the
> conspirators and slain whilst proceeding
> towards the river.[3]

The identity of al-Afdal's assassins remains
disputed, attributed variously to either supporters of the Nizari *da'wa* or al-Amir himself.
Nonetheless, with al-Afdal's demise, the Fatimid
Imam-caliph al-Amir now emerged at the helm
of his state. Among his first acts was the appointment of a new vizier, one who had risen in the
service of the family of Badr al-Jamali.

Born circa 1085, Muhammad b. al-Bata'ihi
was probably an Ithna'ashari Shi'a. In his early
years, he most likely worked as a page in the
Fatimid palace. Tasked with handling precious
items, he received the title *al-Ma'mun* (the
Trustworthy) from the Imam-caliph al-Mustansir,
one by which he would become most known,
and thereafter rose through the ranks to become
one of al-Afdal's most important ministers.

When appointed to the vizierate by al-Amir,
Ma'mun al-Bata'ihi took to his role with gusto.
The ceremonials and public celebrations that once
invigorated Fatimid Cairo, including the birthday
(*mawlid*) celebrations of the Prophet Muhammad,
were restored. The once-thriving Dar al-Ilm,
which had recently become mired in controversy
as a centre for heresy, was reopened at a new location in 1122 and placed under the authority of
an eminent Musta'lian Ismaili *da'i*. Meanwhile,
the project for constructing an astronomical

observatory near Cairo, begun by al-Afdal, was continued by al-Bata'ihi, but remained incomplete, courting controversy for its exorbitant expenditure.

In this renewed milieu of patronage and prosperity, a new cadre of scholarship emerged. Particularly prominent was the Maliki Sunni scholar Abu Bakr Muhammad b. al-Walid, better known as Ibn al-Turtushi (d. 1126). Originally from Catalonia in north-eastern Spain, Ibn al-Turtushi had spent years studying across the Muslim world before settling in Alexandria. His eminent reputation as a teacher of Sunni jurisprudence and *hadith* enhanced the city's reputation as a centre of Sunni scholarship. It was there, in 1122, that Ibn al-Turtushi completed his *Siraj al-Muluk* ('the Lamp of Kings'). A theory of the ideals of Muslim governance in over 64 chapters, the *Siraj* gained renown as one of al-Turtushi's most prized and widely cited works; it was dedicated to the vizier al-Bata'ihi.

The Renewal of Art, Architecture, and the Moonlit Mosque

By the turn of the century, a small but striking building, around 20 metres wide and surmounted by a tower, could be found perched atop the Muqattam escarpment. It was known as the *mashhad* (memorial) of Badr al-Jamali – today, called the *Jami al-Juyushi* (al-Juyushi Mosque) – and its ornate inscriptions honoured al-Mustansir bi'llah and recounted Badr's titles. Its precise function remains debated – whether it was a mosque, a victory memorial, or even a watchtower – but its construction symbolized renewal in the capital.

The return to prosperity ushered in a rejuvenated culture of art and architecture in Egypt, with wealthy patrons embellishing hallowed spaces. Among these was the new *mihrab* (prayer niche) of the Ibn Tulun Mosque. Constructed in 1094 by al-Afdal, the *mihrab* is celebrated as one of the greatest surviving examples of Fatimid stucco work. Standing 3.15 metres high, with Qur'anic verses etched on the main arch, the exquisite geometric patterns and letter-ends derive from a combination of Egyptian and Iranian craftsmanship.

Figure 23. Al-Juyushi Mosque

The monument overlooks the city of Cairo. It was built in 1085 by Badr al-Jamali to celebrate the return of Fatimid order after a series of revolts.

Though the Fatimid enceinte Cairo was by now a built environment, space was nonetheless found for what is today considered the epitome of the Fatimid mosque-building tradition. Drawing on its predecessors in Egypt and Ifriqiya, the mosque

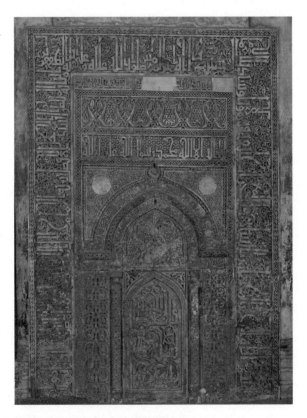

Figure 24. Stucco *Mihrab* in the Ibn Tulun Mosque
This *mihrab* (prayer niche) was commissioned in 1094 by the vizier al-Afdal. It contains the Shi'i *shahada* (profession of faith).

was completed by Ma'mun al-Bata'ihi in 1125 and represents the final act in the trilogy of Fatimid Cairo's mosques, each named after a quality of light: first al-Azhar (the radiant), then al-Anwar (the luminous), and now al-Aqmar (the moonlit).

Built next to the Imam-caliph's palace, the front wall of the al-Aqmar Mosque opened directly onto Cairo's main thoroughfare; behind it, the remainder of the mosque was angled south-eastwards to face Mecca. As the city grew more densely populated over the subsequent centuries, the double orientation of mosques became a characteristic feature of Cairene architectural tradition.

It was al-Aqmar's façade that may have most arrested the attention of worshippers. Decorated with a beautiful constellation of niches and *muqarnas* hoods, its centrepiece was an exquisite stone hood. Inside this hood sat a carved stone medallion inscribed with the names of the Prophet Muhammad and Imam Ali, framed by Q. 33:33 pronouncing the purification of the *ahl al-bayt*: 'God only desires to keep away the uncleanness from you, O people of the House, and to purify you a (thorough) purifying.'

In the swathe of new public buildings and artefacts, inscriptions proclaiming the sovereignty of al-Amir and his father al-Musta'li became ubiquitous. Even though caliphal inscriptions were then commonplace, those of al-Amir and al-Musta'li assumed a particular salience. Almost 30 years had elapsed since the Nizari–Musta'li schism, yet the calls of the Nizari *da'wa* continued to gain momentum in Egypt and Syria.

Figure 25. Façade of al-Aqmar Mosque
The mosque was built by the vizier Ma'mun al-Bata'ihi for the Imam-caliph al-Amir in 1125. The mosque's façade is decorated with stalactites (*muqarnas*), a feature which went on to be specifically found in Muslim religious buildings.

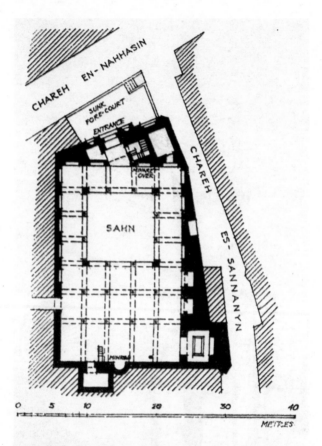

Figure 26. Floor Plan of al-Aqmar Mosque
Floor plan of the mosque of al-Aqmar showing the change in angle allowing
the sanctuary to be aligned towards Mecca. Taken from Creswell, *The Muslim
Architecture of Egypt*, p. 242.

Figure 27. Roundel from the Façade of al-Aqmar Mosque
The roundel shows the names of Muhammad and Ali in the centre.

The Consolidation of the Nizari *Da'wa* in Iran

For almost 70 years after the proclamation of
Nizar's imamate, coins bearing his regnal title
'al-Mustafa li-Din Allah' were minted in parts
of Iran. There, by the early 12th century, several
new fortress regions had coalesced under the
leadership of Alamut to constitute the state of the
Nizari *da'wa*. Among the earliest was the fortress
Lamasar, along the western route to Alamut,
secured in 1096 by *da'i* Kiya Buzurg Ummid, a

Daylami who in time ascended to the Nizari
da'wa leadership. Soon to be included also were
the fortress of Girdukh at the eastern end of the
Alborz mountains, that of Tikrit in Iraq, and that
of Shahdiz found only 8 kilometres south of the
Seljuk capital Isfahan.

Surrounded by Seljuk territories, the fortunes
of the Nizari state were closely tied to those of the
Seljuks. The Nizari state oscillated between cycles
of expansion and contraction as their conflict with
the Seljuks ebbed and flowed. The development of
the Nizari state was complemented by new articulations of the doctrines of the Ismaili imamate,
expressed now in Persian by the *hujja* Hasan-i
Sabbah. The necessity of having a living Imam as
the authoritative leader and guide for humanity
had underpinned the Fatimid Shi'i claim to
authority. Integral to this was the notion of *ta'lim*,
that the Imam's teachings serve as the supreme
means to salvation. The reiteration of this pivotal
Fatimid principle was central to Hasan-i Sabbah's
teaching, and in time it came to be referred to as
al-da'wa al-jadida (the new *da'wa*).

In his famous work, titled the *Four Chapters*
(*chahar fasl* in Persian; *al-fusul al-arba'a* in
Arabic), Hasan-i Sabbah presented the importance of *ta'lim* in living a righteous life through
four extended logical propositions. In summary,
these argued that humankind was incapable of
understanding religious truths through reason
(*aql*) alone, and consequently required instruction from an authoritative teacher (*mu'allim
sadiq*) appointed by God. They concluded with

the proposition that only the living Nizari Ismaili Imam of the time fulfilled this salvific role, with Hasan-i Sabbah asserting the Imam's prerogative of articulating and interpreting doctrines for each time and age.

Such was the centrality of the teaching that the Nizari community at large would be referred to as the Ta'limiya. Its appeal gave rise to a proliferation of rival literature by Sunni scholars who sought to counter the Nizari *da'wa*'s appeal, including that composed by perhaps the most influential Sunni scholar of the medieval age, Abu Hamid al-Ghazali (d. 1111).

The Seljuk Opposition and the Nizari Da'wa in Syria

The conflict between the Nizaris and the Seljuks in Iran reached something of a stalemate, with the Nizaris well defended in their fortress regions and the Seljuks holding Iran's major cities. Clashes continued, however, in local settings. In the early decades of the 1100s, various Seljuk *amir*s executed violent purges against local Nizari communities and their fortresses, often accompanied by bloody massacres, with the Nizari military command retaliating with the assassination of Seljuk officers and preachers who denounced their cause.

In 1124, Hasan-i Sabbah passed away and was succeeded by his trusted lieutenant, Kiya Buzurg Ummid, who ruled over the next 14 years. By now, the Nizari *da'wa* extended to Syria, where it soon became dominant amongst the country's Ismaili populace. Initial successes in Seljuk Aleppo and Damascus were, however, followed by massacres against the Ismailis led by anti-Ismaili elements in the country, causing Syria's Nizari *da'wa* to shift its focus. From the 1130s, the Jabal Bahra mountain range between Homs and the Syrian coast became a site of intense *da'wa* activity, leading to Masyaf Castle becoming a stronghold of the *da'wa* in 1141. In time, the Nizari *da'wa* in Syria would reach its apex under its foremost leader, Rashid al-Din Sinan (d. 1192 or 1193).

Earlier in Egypt, however, the spread of the Nizari *da'wa* had already caused much consternation. Added to rumours spreading that members of the Fatimid household still upheld the claims of Nizar, they culminated in new formal pronouncements on the events of 1094.

Al-Amir's Decree

In December 1122, Egypt's notables gathered at the palace in Cairo. Led by the vizier al-Bata'ihi, they sat in attendance, and awaited a formal pronouncement regarding the succession crisis that had occurred in 1094.

The Egyptian chronicler Ibn al-Muyassar records that an elderly royal princess, a sister of Nizar and al-Musta'li, was also present. Speaking from behind a screen, she related that she had been at Imam-caliph al-Mustansir's deathbed, that the Imam-caliph had spoken with al-Musta'li and then to his own sister – her aunt – to relay the transfer of the *nass*, and that al-Mustansir's sister had announced it to the leading army generals the next day. The royal princess added that Nizar had not rebelled against al-Musta'li, but rather against the unjust treatment meted out by the general al-Afdal. Ibn al-Muyassar concludes:

> Al-Ma'mun [al-Bata'ihi] ordered Ibn al-Sayrafi the *katib* to compose a *sijill* to be read from the pulpit of Fustat.[4]

Called *al-Hidaya al-Amiriyya* ('The Amiri Guidance'), the decree pronounced in the name of the Imam-caliph al-Amir reiterated the appointment of al-Musta'li and disavowed that a descendant of Nizar was living in Iran. It was circulated in Egypt, Syria, and beyond. Shortly thereafter, a rebuttal was composed by the Nizaris of Syria, leading to a further response from the Fatimid court.

The Swansong of the Fatimid Chancery

As a *sijill* of the reigning Imam-caliph, the *Hidaya al-Amiriyya* required composition by an expert hand. It was therefore assigned to the seasoned *katib* Ali b. Munjib b. Sulayman, commonly known as Ibn al-Sayrafi. Ibn al-Sayrafi was born into a wealthy Egyptian family in 1071. He entered the government service whilst young and soon rose in the *diwan al-jaysh*. In 1102, aged 31, he was transferred by al-Afdal to the prestigious *diwan al-insha* and was promoted as its head. His career in the government service spanned 50 years.

As a literary scholar, Ibn al-Sayrafi composed several works, including collections of letters and anthologies of poetry. Of his most famous texts are those that drew on his experience as a Fatimid *katib*, including the *Qanun diwan al-rasa'il* ('Regulations for the Office of Correspondence') that outlined the principles of chancery practice. Most well known, however, is his *al-Ishara ila man nal al-wizara* ('Allusion to Those who Acquired the Vizierate'). Recounting the history of the Egyptian viziers beginning with Ya'qub b. Killis and ending with Ma'mun al-Bata'ihi, it provides insights into the inner workings of the Fatimid government and remains a vital source for historians today.

The Question of Succession

In 1125, the Imam-caliph al-Amir ordered the arrest of Ma'mun al-Bata'ihi and he was executed three years later. The cause remains unclear but is probably connected to a protégé of al-Bata'ihi who escaped to Yemen and proclaimed the continuity of the imamate in Nizar's progeny.

Crises again ensued in October 1130, when the Imam-caliph al-Amir was assassinated. While some pointed fingers at adherents of the Nizari *da'wa*, responsibility remained disputed. In the aftermath, a new question of succession afflicted the Fatimid realms.

The birth of an infant son – al-Tayyib – to the Imam-caliph al-Amir in March 1130 is widely attested. Seemingly an occasion for celebration in Cairo, al-Tayyib's birth was especially marked by adherents of the Musta'lian *da'wa* in Yemen. But when al-Amir died, al-Tayyib was only seven months old, and soon many within the capital deemed it fitting to forget his presence as new powerholders jostled for control.

On the day after al-Amir's passing, a unique enthronement ceremony was held at the palace. Seemingly designed by the two closest ministers of al-Amir, and with the existence of the infant Tayyib ignored, it was pronounced that al-Amir had left behind a pregnant wife. Consequently, it was declared that until the birth of her expected son, Abd al-Majid b. Muhammad – a cousin of al-Amir and grandson of al-Mustansir – would be placed on the throne as a temporary caretaker. Abd al-Majid b. Muhammad was born at Ascalon, sometime between 1073 and 1076, where his father Muhammad – another son of the Imam-caliph al-Mustansir – had been sent for safety during the *shidda*. Having since then returned to Cairo, he was in his 50s when al-Amir's ministers appointed him head of the Fatimid state.

Soon thereafter, a scion of Badr al-Jamali's family stepped up to seize power. Abu Ali Ahmad, nicknamed Kutayfat, was a son of al-Afdal. With the support of the *juyushiyya*, Kutayfat arrested Abd al-Majid b. Muhammad and took the unprecedented step of declaring the imamate of the awaited *mahdi* in the Ithna'ashari tradition, on whose behalf he was now ruling as a representative. As expected, the annulment of the Fatimid claim caused severe consternation in the capital's Ismaili circles. A year later, in December 1131, officers in the Fatimid army, supported by the adherents of al-Amir, removed Kutayfat, ending the final flourish of the Jamali family.

The Hafizi *Dawla*

The killing of Kutayfat saw the freeing of Abd al-Majid b. Muhammad and his return to the throne as temporary regent. In March 1132, however, another novel milestone in the Fatimid age was passed. *Sijill*s from the Fatimid chancery pronounced that Abd al-Majid b. Muhammad was himself the new Imam-caliph and bestowed on him the regnal title *al-Hafiz li-Din Allah* (the Preserver of the Religion of God).

Hitherto, the passing of the imamate from father to son had been a cardinal principle of the Fatimid dynasty that was rooted in Imami Shi'i doctrine. With al-Hafiz being declared Imam-caliph, however, cousin-to-cousin succession became legitimized. Here, al-Hafiz had appealed to the founding precedent in Shi'i Islam – the designation by the Prophet Muhammad of his own cousin, Ali b. Abi Talib, as his successor at Ghadir Khumm in 632. For the new Hafizi *da'wa*, just as the *nass* had passed from the Prophet to his cousin Ali, it now passed from al-Amir to his cousin al-Hafiz. The language of the state transformed accordingly, and the *kuttab* of the chancellery now spoke of *al-dawla al-Hafiziyya* (the Hafizi state), based on *al-imama al-Hafiziyya* (the Hafizi imamate).

The Imam-caliph al-Hafiz would rule for 17 years, and he would be the last Fatimid ruler to be proclaimed Imam-caliph as an adult. While there were periods of stability and even prosperity during his reign, it was clear that the grip of the military factions on Egypt could not be unclasped.

The first upheavals came unexpectedly from al-Hafiz's own son. Seeking to shift power away from ministers and generals towards his own household, the Imam-caliph had promoted his sons to the highest offices of state. Rivalries erupted when another son, Hasan b. al-Hafiz, gathered armies to secure his own promotion in 1135. The whole affair turned especially bloody when he embarked on murderous purges to eliminate rivals. When officers gathered at the palace demanding Hasan's head in 1135, the Imam-caliph al-Hafiz was forced to order his son's death.

Meanwhile, Bahram – a Christian governor of Egypt who came from a princely Armenian family – had brought his own army to Cairo in support of Hasan b. al-Hafiz, and he soon took control of the capital. Bahram's recruitment of Christian Armenians and links with the Crusaders and other Christian kingdoms fuelled sectarian fervour. Many Muslims reacted against what they saw as an effort to establish Christian rule. Their champion came in the form of Ridwan al-Walakshi. Ridwan was a Sunni general of the Fatimid army who had served as al-Hafiz's jailer during the short reign of Kutayfat. He defeated Bahram in 1137 and then anointed himself *al-Malik* (the King). Ridwan seemingly sought to end al-Hafiz's caliphate, until in 1139 Ridwan was deposed. Finally, from 1139 to 1149 the

Imam-caliph al-Hafiz reigned as the Fatimid sovereign, though his rule was beset by continued factional fighting in the capital. Among the notable features of his period was the renewal of patronage of the shrines of the *ahl al-bayt*.

The Shrines of the Ahl al-Bayt

The Qarafa had long been a repository of sacred spaces for Egypt's inhabitants. Constituting its symbolic core were a series of tombs of some of the descendants of the Prophet Muhammad, through the line of Ali b. Abi Talib and Fatima al-Zahra, who had died in Egypt. Among them were particularly esteemed descendants of the early Shiʿi Imams, whose tombs served as gravitational centres around which the graves of other members of Egypt's *ashraf* were clustered. Forming a constellation of sacrality and a locus of prophetic *baraka*, they served as places of visitation and prayer for the Shiʿa and Sunnis alike. During the reigns of al-Amir and al-Hafiz, the tombs benefitted from a new programme of building and renewal. Today, they remain the largest group of tomb monuments that survive from the first six centuries of Muslim history.

The tomb of Umm Kulthum bt. Muhammad was well known amongst those of the Qarafa. Umm Kulthum was the great-granddaughter of Imam Jaʿfar al-Sadiq. She had migrated to Egypt alongside her father and brothers and there passed away in 868. Her tomb had first been built by patrons from Egypt's pre-Fatimid period. In 1122 it was renewed under the patronage of

the vizier Ma'mun al-Bata'ihi, its new *mihrab*
recurrently projecting the names of the Prophet
Muhammad and Imam Ali. Close by lay the
resting places of her father, Abu Tayyib al-Qasim,
the grandson of Imam Ja'far al-Sadiq, and her
brothers Muhammad (d. 875) and Yahya (d. 877),
whose tombs were also renewed during this
time.

In the first years of al-Hafiz's reign in 1133,
another esteemed tomb saw renewal, that of
al-Sayyida Ruqayya, an attested daughter of Imam
Ali b. Abi Talib. Patronized this time by a widow
of the Imam-caliph al-Amir, the tomb's renovation included the construction of a triple series of
*mihrab*s on its *qibla* wall (the wall facing Mecca).
In 1138, the Imam-caliph al-Hafiz himself patronized the revitalization of the tomb of al-Sayyida
Nafisa (d. 824). Nafisa was a descendant of the
Imam al-Hasan b. Ali b. Abi Talib. Famed amongst
Egypt's luminaries, and as a female scholar in her
own right, she had gained renown in the country
as a teacher of prophetic traditions, notably
being among those from whom the Sunni jurist
al-Shafi'i had come to learn. The period also
saw the construction of new tombs, with al-Hafiz
building a new shrine for al-Sayyida Maryam, a
descendant of the Tabataba family that stemmed
from the line of Imam al-Hasan b. Ali and were
among the most notable members of the *ashraf* in
Egypt.

The Fatimids' programme of the renewal and
construction of tombs in the 1100s has been
understood by historians as a means of reinforcing

Figure 28. Portable *Mihrab*
Portable, wooden *mihrab* (built ca. 1154–1160) from the Tomb of Sayyida Ruqayya.

Figure 29. Tomb of Sayyida Ruqayya
The building was constructed in 1133 as a memorial to Sayyida Ruqayya on the orders of Imam-caliph al-Hafiz.

Figure 30. Sayyida Nafisa Mosque
Sayyida Nafisa (along with Sayyida Ruqayya) is considered a patron saint of the
city of Cairo. Her mosque-shrine complex is a popular site for the performance
of Sufi rituals, as well as for weddings and celebrations.

belief in the sanctity of the family of the Prophet,
which was important in an era where contesting
claims to the Fatimid imamate had brought questions of legitimacy to the fore. Symbolizing this
proclaimed sanctity was the repeated use of
Qur'anic verses on the tombs, including the Verse
of Light (Q. 2:255) and especially the Verse of
Purification (Q. 33:33) where God pronounced the
distinct purification of the *ahl al-bayt*.

The Tayyibi *Da'wa* in Yemen

As a gateway to the Red Sea and the Indian
Ocean, Yemen remained valuable to the Fatimid
state in Egypt in the 12th century. In 1119, during

the height of Arwa's regency, the *amir al-juyush* al-Afdal had sought to bolster the Yemeni *da'wa* but also assert Cairo's control by sending a direct representative, Ali b. Najib al-Dawla, to Yemen ostensibly in support of Arwa. Ali was initially successful in helping the Sulayhids in Yemen, but even though aided by soldiers and supplies, this became fraught with difficulty. Soon thereafter, Ali was forced to return to Cairo, where he was then executed in 1128, in the same year as Ma'mun al-Bata'ihi. Both had been accused of loyalties to the descendants of Nizar.

Two years later, the news reached Yemen that the Imam-caliph al-Amir had passed away. For Arwa al-Sulayhi and the Musta'lians of Yemen, the issue of succession was already settled. By then, according to the Yemeni Ismaili tradition, a letter dictated by al-Amir had already circulated amongst them, announcing the birth in March 1130 of al-Amir's son al-Tayyib, who he had declared the *wali al-ahd*. When al-Amir died in October, Yemen's *da'wa* under the Sulayhids pronounced its allegiance to al-Tayyib. Regarding the infant Imam's fate, it was declared that turbulence in Cairo necessitated the concealment of al-Tayyib, and that his father's closest supporters had escorted him to safety, where he remained in concealment. This concealment marked the beginning of a new *dawr al-satr*, one that continues to this day according to the doctrines of the Tayyibi *da'wa*. The *da'wa*'s doctrine upheld that al-Tayyib grew into adulthood and fathered his own progeny, who remain in concealment and in whom the line of the imamate continues. Yemen thus became the heartland of the now Tayyibi Ismaili community, and it sought to strengthen its mission amongst the Ismailis of India.

Having broken off all ties with the Hafizi state in Egypt, Arwa al-Sulayhi devoted her twilight years to consolidating the Tayyibi *da'wa*. In the new era of *satr*, she instituted the office of *da'i al-mutlaq* (the Absolute *da'i*), in which the incumbent would serve as the deputy of the concealed Tayyibi Imam. In 1132, the first *da'i al-mutlaq* was appointed: al-Dhu'ayb b. Musa al-Wadi'i, the erudite *da'i* and then head of the Musta'lian *da'wa* in Yemen. Arwa continued to support the Tayyibi cause until her passing in 1138. She was buried in the mosque that she had consecrated in Dhu Jibla. Retaining influences of Fatimid architecture, the tomb-mosque complex remains a hallowed site of pilgrimage for the Tayyibi Ismailis today.

With Yemen then also long shaped by tribal politics, Arwa's declaration of allegiance to Tayyib was not, however, ubiquitous amongst its Ismaili communities. By the time of al-Amir's passing, semi-independent rulers from within the *da'wa* had already established strongholds in Sana'a and Aden, though ostensibly under Sulayhid suzerainty. In Aden, a vital port-city that prospered on the Red Sea and Indian Ocean trade, members of the Zuray'ids of the Banu Hamdan had long challenged Arwa's supremacy. With the declaration of al-Hafiz's imamate, the leaders of Sana'a and the Zuray'ids of Aden pronounced their allegiance to al-Hafiz. Prospering from the continuing richness of Red Sea trade and increasingly supported by the Hafizi *dawla* due to Aden's strategic importance, the now independent Zuray'ids would remain ardent followers of the Hafizi *da'wa*, and Aden became the last significant outpost of Fatimid sovereignty outside Egypt.

The Finale of Fatimid Rule

In 1149, now in his 70s, the Imam-caliph al-Hafiz passed away. With his four eldest sons having predeceased him, al-Hafiz had appointed as his successor his son Ismail, who took the regnal name *al-Zafir bi-Amr Allah* (the Victorious by God's Command).

Born in 1133, al-Zafir was aged 16 when his reign began. It did so amidst recurring factional fighting between Turkish and Nubian troops and was soon, additionally, plagued by some of the most notorious figures of medieval Muslim history. Personal rivalries fuelled rebellions led by the governor of Alexandria, al-Adil b. al-Sallar, and his stepson Abbas b. Abi'l-Futuh. It resulted in each taking control of Cairo in 1149 and 1154, respectively. Ibn al-Sallar gained renown for his military prowess but also infamy for his brutality, not least for his massacre of the Fatimid army's cadet corps (*sibyan al-khass*), which he suspected of planning a coup. Abbas b. Abi'l-Futuh was no less infamous. Having instigated the assassination of his once ally and stepfather Ibn al-Sallar, in 1153 Abbas b. Abi'l-Futuh gained the vizierate. Spurred by rumours that his own son Nasr was involved in a relationship with al-Zafir, Abbas had his son kill the young Imam-caliph in March 1154 having first lured al-Zafir outside the palace grounds.

Succession was once again decided by Cairo's latest military ruler. Isa, the five-year-old son of al-Zafir, was pronounced the next Fatimid Imam-caliph with the regnal name *al-Fa'iz bi-Nasr Allah* (the Triumphant with the Help of God). The chroniclers relate that the young al-Fa'iz, seeing the corpses of his uncles gruesomely displayed after they had been falsely accused of killing al-Zafir, and then being subjected to loud cries of obedience by the soldiers of Abbas b. Abi'l-Futuh, was afflicted by mental trauma from which he would never recover. The dissolution of the caliphal power of the Hafizi *dawla* seemed inevitable. Yet there was to be a final flourish of stable and centralized Shi'i authority in the Fatimid domains.

The Black Banners of al-Salih Tala'i

In July 1154, an army of soldiers gathered outside Cairo carrying black banners, a symbol of their mourning and their claim to vengeance for the massacred sons of al-Hafiz. Leading the army was the general Tala'i b. Ruzzik, whom the chronicles relate had been summoned by the women of the Fatimid household to save the Hafizi dynasty.

Though his origins are unclear, Tala'i b. Ruzzik was probably born around 1101 or 1102 to an Armenian officer who had come to Egypt with Badr al-Jamali. A convert to Twelver Shi'ism,

Tala'i had risen through the ranks of the Fatimid army until, in his fifties, he was appointed governor of Asyut in Upper Egypt. Now camped outside Cairo in 1154 and seeking vengeance, Tala'i's presence caused Abbas b. Abi'l-Futuh to flee. The ex-vizier looted the Fatimid treasury before escaping, only to be later captured with the stolen possessions in Crusader territory.

With his successful entry into Cairo, Tala'i b. Ruzzik adopted the title *al-Malik al-Salih* (the Virtuous King). The legacy of his vizierate was long disputed. Historians like Ibn Khallikan and Ibn Zafir castigated him for his violence, cata- lysed by his zealous anti-Sunnism, and for his unscrupulous gathering of wealth. Others like Ibn Sa'id al-Andalusi listed him alongside Ya'qub b. Killis and al-Afdal b. Badr as one of the great Fatimid viziers. Al-Salih al-Tala'i – as he was henceforth called – was, however, undoubtedly the last of the Fatimid viziers to uphold Fatimid Egypt as an independent Shi'i power.

The Shrine of al-Husayn b. Ali in Cairo

For over 50 years, a remarkable, and still surviv- ing, wooden pulpit (*minbar*) sat within a famed shrine of Fatimid Ascalon – the shrine containing the head (*ra's*) of the grandson of the Prophet, the Imam al-Husayn b. Ali b. Abi Talib.

According to tradition, while the body of Imam al-Husayn lay at the battlefield of Karbala where he had been killed by Umayyad forces in 680, his head had been taken by the Umayyads to Syria in triumph. While the general Shi'i tradition

Figure 31. The Cenotaph of al-Husayn
The head of al-Husayn was brought from Ascalon to Cairo for safety in 1153 where it was reinterred near the graves of the Fatimid ancestors, around 500 metres from the Eastern Palace.

held that al-Husayn's head had been reinterred with his body, traditions proclaiming the head's continued presence in Syria still circulated. In 1091, upon the basis of a miracle, the vizier Badr al-Jamali claimed the discovery of the resting place of the head of al-Husayn in Fatimid Ascalon. Memorializing his rise to power, the vizier built a shrine (*mashhad*) for the head in Ascalon, turning the port-city into a place of pilgrimage for the Shiʻi faithful. Other accounts attribute the discovery and construction of the shrine to al-Afdal.

Figure 32. The Ayyubid Minaret above the Tomb of the Head of al-Husayn
The location of the cenotaph of the head of al-Husayn is the *Bab al-Akhdar* (the
Green Gate). In 1237, the Ayyubids built a minaret above this gate, and then in
the late 19th century Khedive Ismail had the surrounding mosque reconstruc-
ted in the Italian Gothic style with the addition of Ottoman-style pencil
minarets, almost completely subsuming the site of the cenotaph.

For decades, the fortress-city of Ascalon had stood as Fatimid Egypt's last line of defence against the Crusaders, but by 1153 Ascalon was at the cusp of falling following a long Crusader siege. During the negotiated evacuation of the city, the head of al-Husayn was removed and carried westwards, where in Cairo it soon found a new resting place.

The Saffron Tomb (*Turbat al-Za'faran*) to the south of Cairo's palace had, since the city's foundation, been the hallowed space of the Fatimid dynasty. There, the Imam-caliphs from al-Mahdi bi'llah to al-Mu'izz and their successors had been laid to rest and halting at the tomb was an integral part of the Fatimid procession ceremonies. To the east of the Saffron Tomb, considered apposite as a sacred location for a forefather of the Fatimids, the martyrium for al-Husayn's head was established. Thirty years later, in Egypt – now ruled by the Sunni successor dynasty of the Ayyubids – the geographer Ibn Jubayr (d. 1217) came to the shrine:

> We observed men kissing the blessed tomb, surrounding it, throwing themselves upon it, smoothing with their hands the *kiswa* that was over it, moving round it in a surging throng, calling out invocations, weeping and entreating Glorious God to bless the hallowed dust, such as would melt the heart and split the hardest flint. A solemn thing it was, an awe-inspiring insight.[5]

In 1161, al-Salih al-Tala'i then patronized the construction of the last great mosque of Fatimid Cairo. Built just beyond Cairo's southern gate, the Mosque of al-Salih al-Tala'i was the first of Cairo's suspended mosques. Common in later dynasties and especially in the Ottoman realms, suspended mosques were built upon a raised platform beneath which existed rows of shops, the rents of which were ordained as endowments (*waqfs*) for the mosque's upkeep. Repaired and renovated by successive dynasties, the Mosque of al-Salih al-Tala'i remains today as one of the final surviving constructions of Fatimid Egypt.

Figure 33. The Mosque of al-Salih al-Tala'i
The last major Fatimid monument, the mosque was built by al-Salih al-Tala'i in 1161. The whole mosque was built on a platform, and at ground-floor level three of the sides contain recesses for shops to generate income for the mosque.

Renewed Celebrations of the Festival of al-Ghadir

In 1161, Talaʾi oversaw a new succession ceremony to the Fatimid throne. Ever suffering from
the trauma of his childhood, the young Hafizi
Imam-caliph al-Faʾiz died aged 11 in 1160. As
al-Faʾiz had no offspring, the precedent of cousin-
to-cousin succession was resurrected. A grandson
of al-Hafiz known as Abdallah b. Yusuf was chosen.
Aged 9, he acceded to office with the regnal title
al-Adid li-Din Allah (the Supporter of God's
Religion), and he would be the last Imam-caliph of
the Fatimid age. For the adherents of the Hafizi
daʿwa, the principle of cousin-to-cousin succession
catalysed the renewal of one of the most important
public celebrations of the Fatimid calendar – Eid
al-Ghadir (the festival of al-Ghadir).

Marking the day in the year 632 when, according to Shiʿi doctrine, the Prophet pronounced
Ali b. Abi Talib his successor at Ghadir Khumm,
the celebrations of Eid al-Ghadir had been a
feature of ritual life in Fatimid Cairo. From
as early as 973, the first year of Imam-caliph
al-Muʿizz's arrival in Egypt, celebrations of
the day of Ghadir (*yawm al-ghadir*) entered
into the annual calendar, as relayed by Ibn
Zulaq:

> On 18 Dhu'l-Hijja (19 September 973), the
> day of Ghadir Khumm, a group of people
> from Egypt and the Maghrib gathered for
> prayers. Al-Muʿizz appreciated this, and it
> was the first time Id al-Ghadir was celebrated
> in Egypt.[6]

The celebrations of Ghadir Khumm continued thereafter and, being so central to Imami Shiʻi doctrine and identity, they were often led by the Shiʻi faithful themselves. The festival's popularity amongst Cairo's inhabitants is noted by al-Musabbihi, probably during the reign of al-Hakim, when thronging crowds came to celebrate it in the al-Azhar Mosque:

> And on *Yawm al-Ghadir* ... the people gathered in the congregational mosque of Cairo (i.e. al-Azhar), including the Qur'an reciters, the jurists, and the chanters. It was a great gathering (of people), who remained there till the noon-prayer. Then they headed toward the palace, from where rewards were given to them.[7]

In the time of the Hafizi *dawla*, the ceremonies of Eid al-Ghadir took on new significance. It was sometime after 1154, probably during the reigns of either al-Faʼiz or al-Adid, that the grounds of Cairo's great palace complex witnessed the ritual processions to mark the day. Ibn al-Tuwayr (d. 1220), whose career spanned the final years of the Fatimids, relates that as part of the celebrations, the vizier would appear at the Golden Gate of the palace, where the young Imam-caliph would emerge to be greeted and receive homage. Thereafter, a grand parade consisting of cavalry, archers, and infantrymen would proceed. The Imam-caliph's procession would then make its way to the *mashhad* of Imam al-Husayn, where the judges and legal officials were waiting, before entering the great audience hall which had been specially decorated. There, in audience, would be sitting the major Shiʻi figures of the state and the army, and upon the pulpit, the preacher would read from

> a notebook prepared in the *diwan al-insha*, [this] affirming the explicit designation (*nass*) of the Caliphate from the Prophet Muhammad, God's Blessings and Peace be upon him, to the Commander of the Believers, Ali b. Abi Talib, may God ennoble his face.[8]

The Last Imam-Caliph and the Last Vizier

In 1161, a year after al-Adid's accession as Imam-caliph, al-Salih al-Talaʾi was killed, allegedly on the orders of al-Adid's aunt, who had been angered at his dominance over palace affairs. His son Ruzzik b. Talaʾi stepped into his shoes but was himself overthrown two years later. With that, the line of the great Fatimid Armenian viziers came to an end. A new struggle erupted for control of Cairo, this time through the direct involvement of neighbouring dynasties.

It was Shawar b. Munjid al-Saʻdi, governor of Upper Egypt, who had marched his armies to Cairo – probably at the behest of al-Adid's family – and deposed Ruzzik b. Talaʾi in 1163. But Shawar had no sooner established himself as vizier than he was ousted by a new rival – the Fatimid general Dirgham. Dirgham, like Shawar, was of Arab tribal origin, and he had gained renown and a personal following after his victories against the Crusaders in 1158. The exiled governor Shawar was undeterred by his removal, however, and he made his way eastwards to Damascus, seeking audience with the now powerful sultan of the Zengid dynasty.

The Zengid dynasty had emerged as Syria's dominant power by the 1160s, having inflicted major defeats on Crusader armies. Thereafter, the struggle for supremacy between the Zengids and the Crusaders also played out at the Fatimid court, as both turned their eyes towards the rich prize of Fatimid Egypt.

Shawar's arrival in Damascus in 1163 presented an ideal opportunity for the Zengid sultan, Nur al-Din (d. 1174). Under the guise of helping Shawar regain his post as Fatimid vizier, the sultan sent into Egypt a Zengid army led by one of his most noted officers – the Kurdish general Asad al-Din Shirkuh. Upon defeating Dirgham, the Zengids restored Shawar to his position as Fatimid vizier.

The Crusaders reacted with alarm to this development. Loath to have their rivals control Egypt, they soon embarked on their own invasions of Egypt. Between 1164 and 1168, a convoluted struggle unfolded as both powers tried to outdo each other. In Cairo, the rival viziers themselves often switched sides.

The rivalries climaxed in 1168, when a major invasion of the Crusader armies reached the gates of Cairo. Unable to defend the nearby city of Fustat, the vizier Shawar ordered it to be set alight. He then turned once more to the Zengid army for aid. The third and final Zengid invasion of Egypt began. The Crusaders quickly lifted their siege, and the Zengid general Shirkuh entered Cairo unopposed. When the vizier Shawar was killed soon thereafter, the young Imam-caliph al-Adid – unable to oppose Zengid power – formally declared Shirkuh the Fatimid vizier and *amir al-juyush* in 1169.

For the first time in Fatimid Cairo, an officer of an external power stood at the helm of the Fatimid state. Shirkuh's reign as Fatimid vizier was short-lived, however, as he passed away from a quick illness. Power over Cairo then passed to Shirkuh's own nephew, Salah al-Din Yusuf b. Ayyub.

Salah al-Din (born in 1138) is amongst the most well-known figures of the medieval Muslim world. Known in European literature as Saladin, he gained renown in Sunni historiography for his victories against the Crusaders, for ending Shi'i rule in Egypt, and for founding the first successor state of the Fatimids – that of the Ayyubids (1171–1260).

For just over two years, between March 1169 and September 1171, Salah al-Din reigned as Fatimid vizier; like previous occupants of the office, he took a new title, in this case *al-Malik al-Nasir* (the Supporter King). His first objective was eliminating rival blocs of power in the Fatimid realms. Street battles erupted between the Zengid forces and the last surviving battalions of the Fatimid armies, notably the Sudanese infantry; the latter were soon eliminated.

Thereafter, Salah al-Din turned to his principal objective: dismantling the foundations of Fatimid rule. He gave the position of chief judge to a Sunni *qadi*, who dismissed all Shi'i *qadi*s from their posts. The Shi'i form of the *adhan* (call to prayer) was abandoned, and the *majalis al-hikma* were shut down. In September 1171, Salah al-Din ordered the name of the Abbasid caliph to be pronounced – for the first time in just over 200 years – in the sermons of Egypt. With this, Fatimid rule in Egypt came to an end. The last Hafizi Imam-caliph al-Adid would die a little while later; being confined to the palace and cut off from outside developments, he passed away unaware that the time of his *dawla* had turned.

Conclusion: Glimpses of the Fatimid Legacy

> He [al-Muʿizz li-Din Allah] entered Cairo accompanied by all those who had gone [earlier] to receive him, along with all his sons, brothers, paternal uncles, and the rest of the sons of al-Mahdi. The coffins of his ancestors, al-Mahdi, al-Qaʾim and al-Mansur, were also brought with him. His entry into Cairo and his arrival at his palace took place on Tuesday, 7 Ramadan 362 [11 June 973]. Thus, Egypt, after having been the seat of an amirate, became the seat of a caliphate.[1]

Al-Maqrizi's description of al-Muʿizz's arrival in Egypt provides a glimpse of the Fatimid legacy from the perspective of a Sunni Egyptian historian writing over 400 years later. Egypt had been ruled for over a millennium by external powers. However, the Fatimid settlement established the country's independence and cultivated its distinct social, cultural, and intellectual élan. These foundations paved the way for successive Sunni dynasties that reigned from Egypt – from the Ayyubids (1171–1260) to the Mamluks (1250–1517) – from al-Maqrizi's own time.

Modern historians often question how the Fatimids survived late into the 12th century given their preceding tribulations. Among the suggested antidotes is the durability of the Fatimid model of governance. This model allowed people from diverse religious and ethnic backgrounds to participate in a complex state apparatus. The participants not only provided wide-ranging competencies from across the Muslim, Christian, and Jewish communities, but also gained from their own investment in the progression of the Fatimid state.

The administrative endurance of the Fatimid state during its final tumultuous decades reflected this robustness. While political and natural disasters took their toll, the governmental apparatus had developed the wherewithal for regeneration. The long careers of government officials, such as the 50-year employment of Ibn al-Sayrafi, testifies to this resilience.

A coterie of Egyptian officials who had risen in the Fatimid administration subsequently transitioned into the Ayyubid one, enabling a continuity of administrative expertise. Al-Qadi al-Fadil was one such figure. He was born in 1135 in Ascalon and enrolled as a trainee in the Fatimid *diwan al-insha*, where he became its director before he had turned 40. When Salah al-Din ended Fatimid rule, he turned to al-Fadil who, over the next 22 years, gained fame as secretary and chief counsellor to Egypt's new sultan. Following Salah al-Din's death in 1193, al-Fadil was retained by his successors. The strength of the Fatimid governmental legacy continued to be recognized centuries later. It was while serving as a senior official in the Mamluk administration that al-Maqrizi composed his works on the Fatimids, probably showcasing their model of Egyptian governance as a source of emulation for the sovereigns of his own age.

*   *   *

The only Shi'i dynasty to reign over Egypt, the Fatimids galvanized an abiding veneration for the *ahl al-bayt* in the Egyptian psyche. While Cairo's palace complex disappeared soon after the passing of the Fatimid state, the sacred enclaves of the royal tomb containing the resting place of Imam al-Husayn's head were protected. The tomb of the head of Imam al-Husayn remains among Egypt's most holy spaces – a place for pilgrimage, prayer, and contemplation for those seeking the *baraka* of the *ahl al-bayt*. Today, over a million men, women, and children from across Egypt converge on Cairo every year to mark Imam Husayn's birthday, offering their prayers and seeking the intercession of the beloved grandson of the Prophet.

The Fatimid legacy also permeates Egyptian ritual life. The annual *mawlid* celebrations of the Prophet Muhammad were first commemorated by the Fatimids and remain an integral feature of Egypt's ritual calendar. The veneration of the *ahl al-bayt* transcends the Sunni–Shi'i divide. Expressions of attachment to the Prophet and his *ahl al-bayt* remain vital features of the devotional

Figure 34. Members of the Shadhiliyya *Tariqa*
During the celebrations of *mawlid al-nabi* (the Prophet's birthday), throngs of
Sufi orders assemble in temporary tented structures outside the mosque of
al-Husayn, where they sit until the early hours listening to sermons and
devotional poems sung in praise of the Prophet.

practice of Egypt's Muslims, especially among
the country's Sufis, which conservative estimates
place at over 15 million, with some 75 Sufi orders
(*tariqas*) giving expression to the spiritual aspirations of its practitioners.

* * *

For Ismaili Shi'i communities today, the
two-century Fatimid heritage is ingrained in their
history and psyche: an era when their Imams
reigned over a vast empire, where their *da'is* and
scholars were at the forefront of intellectual
discourse in the Muslim world, and whose vast

literary output strengthened the doctrinal articulations of faith.

Both Nizari and Tayyibi Ismaili communities today view themselves as heirs to Fatimid history. For them, Egypt evokes a living legacy, with surviving Fatimid monuments and literature as testament of their inheritance. Egypt is remembered as the homeland of many of their Imams, and as the intellectual and cultural hub of their empire, albeit over a millennium ago. For the Nizari Ismailis it also marks, more recently, the resting place of their 48th Imam, Mawlana Sultan Mahomed Shah (d. 1957), buried by the scenic banks of the Nile in Aswan, and whose mausoleum bears the imprint of Fatimid architecture.

Figure 35. The Mausoleum of Aga Khan III Overlooking the Nile at Aswan
The mausoleum of Sir Sultan, Mahomed Shah, Aga Khan III, built on a hilltop overlooking the Nile at Aswan, where he liked to spend time in the winter 'in the land of his forefathers'.

For Tayyibi Ismailis the visitation of Fatimid mosques and monuments is amongst the meritorious acts embarked on by the faithful, as is participation in the restoration of Fatimid sites. These include, among many others, the extensive renovation in 1980 of al-Anwar, the mosque of Imam-caliph al-Hakim bi-Amr Allah, by Syedna Mohammed Burhanuddin (d. 2014), the late head and 52nd *da'i al-mutlaq* of the Tayyibi Ismaili Dawoodi Bohras.

*   *   *

As Africa's largest city and the Arab world's most populous, Cairo retains its distinctive global stature. Since its foundation by the Fatimids, it has stood as Egypt's political, social, cultural, and intellectual heartland. It also serves as a nexus where discourses between the past and the present define everyday life. The city's streets are dotted with buildings and monuments from its Fatimid past, including most famously the al-Azhar mosque–university complex. Its array of quarters and famed monumental buildings likewise display the contributions of successive dynasties who often built alongside or upon their predecessors' edifices – a process perhaps best symbolized by the rounded Mamluk domes added to the Fatimid minarets of the al-Hakim Mosque.

In 1984, a conference held in Cairo sparked a two-decade effort to transform one of the city's oldest quarters, the Darb al-Ahmar, with discussions gravitating around the dialectic between a historic past and a lived present. Amongst the conference delegates was Prince Shah Karim al-Husseini Aga Khan, the 49th Imam of the Nizari Ismailis. Thereafter, under the rubric of the Aga Khan Development Network (AKDN), a major socio-economic regeneration project was initiated, culminating in the construction of al-Azhar Park, affectionately labelled the 'lungs of Cairo', which is one of Cairo's largest open green spaces today.

Once a site of Fatimid and Ayyubid cemeteries, the *Darb al-Ahmar* (the Red Road) became a site of several neighbourhoods, mosque complexes, palaces, and hospitals in the Mamluk era. In the mid-20th century, however, it was a site of economic deprivation. Yet despite the line of dilapidated homes leaning against crumbling monuments, the area remained home to a vibrant community, inhabited often by skilled craftsmen. The proposed development of al-Azhar Park focussed on an area in the Darb al-Ahmar that had for centuries served as a wasteland and dumping ground. The pivotal issue facing the project, however, concerned the question of how a historic site can be renovated in tandem with the aspirations of its local inhabitants?

For those living in the Darb al-Ahmar this was a pressing concern. 'Reverence of the past' had often wrought negative consequences, not least from moratoriums against the repair of living quarters, policies ostensibly designed to preserve heritage sites. Similarly problematic were the potential pitfalls associated with tourism and gentrification. The solution proposed was to harness the past as a medium for sustainable development – to make use of local labour, knowledge, and craftsmanship in the regeneration of both the area and its living conditions – resulting in the construction of al-Azhar Park.

During the excavations, a long-buried segment of an Ayyubid wall was uncovered, built by the very dynasty that had displaced the Fatimids. Incorporated into the park, its discovery and restoration serve as a tangible testament of the dialectic between the past and the present. At his inaugural speech to mark the opening of al-Azhar Park on 25 March 2005, the Aga Khan said:

> In our excavations and our historical investigations [for the park], I constantly have been reminded that we were touching the very foundations of my ancestors, the Fatimids, and the pluralistic history and intellectual profile of this city and this country to which they contributed so profoundly. I am very humbled by the opportunity to return to Cairo, founded over a thousand years ago by the Fatimid caliph Al-Muizz, to build on that history. Thirty-five generations later, through the work done here by my institutions, it is my prayer that this park will be a continuing contribution to the people of this great city.[2]

Glossary

Abbasids	Major Muslim dynasty of caliphs who ruled from Baghdad (750–1258).
ahl al-bayt	Lit. 'people of the house'. In the Prophet's time, the term referred to the Prophet's clan, the Banu Hashim, and – associated with them – the Banu'l-Muttalib. Over the following centuries, the term remained in circulation with various interpretations, until it finally came to mean the progeny of Imam Ali and Fatima (the Prophet Muhammad's daughter).
Ali b. Abi Talib	Cousin of the Prophet, and his son-in-law by marriage to his daughter Fatima; first Shi'i Imam and fourth caliph (d. 661). His descendants became known as the Alids.
amir al-juyush	'Commander of the armies'.
amir al-mu'minin	'Commander of the faithful.' A title used by Muslim caliphs from the seventh century onwards. It is used by the Shi'a for Ali b. Abi Talib and by the Ismailis for the Fatimid Imam-caliphs.
ashraf sing. *sharif*	Nobility. Used initially to denote the chiefs of Arabian tribes, by the

	10th century it denoted the descend- ants of the Prophet Muhammad through Ali and Fatima.
Ayyubids	Sunni dynasty that succeeded the Fatimids (1171–1260), founded by Salah al-Din Yusuf (Saladin).
Buyids	Shi'i dynasty of Iran and Iraq (945–1055) of Daylami origin.
Byzantines	Successor state of the Roman Empire. The Eastern Roman Empire based in Constantinople, generally dated from the 4th to the 15th century.
Copts	Indigenous Christian community of Egypt who spoke Coptic, and probably formed the majority of Egypt's rural populace in the 10th century.
da'i	'Summoner' or 'inviter'. Can be approximated to 'missionary' and denotes an emissary or propagator of the faith. In the hierarchy of the Fatimid da'wa, it represents a specific rank.
da'wa	Mission or invitation. Ismailis often referred to their movement as simply al-da'wa or al-da'wa al-hadiya (the rightly guided call).
dawla	'Turn' or 'alternation', denoting a state or dynasty.
dawlat al-haqq	'The righteous reign'; a term that the Fatimids used to describe their state.
dawr al-satr	'Period of concealment'. Refers to the century-and-a-half during which the Ismaili Imams were hidden from

public knowledge, and which ended with the appearance of Abd Allah al-Mahdi in 909.

Druze A religious movement that arose from elements within the Fatimid *da'wa* and subsequently formed a distinct religious confession.

Eid al-Adha 'Festival of the Sacrifice'. Also called *Eid al-Qurban* or *Eid al-Nahr*. It is celebrated on 10 Dhu'l-Hijja in the Muslim calendar.

Eid al-Fitr 'Festival of the Breaking of the Fast', marking the end of Ramadan.

Eid al-Ghadir 'Festival of Ghadir'. It marks for the Imami Shi'a the Prophet's appointment (*nass*) of Ali b. Abi Talib as his successor in 632 and is celebrated on 18 Dhu'l-Hijja in the Muslim calendar.

Fatimids Major Muslim dynasty of Ismaili caliphs in North Africa (from 909) and later in Egypt (973–1171). The Fatimids claimed descent from the Prophet Muhammad through Ali and derived their name from the Prophet's daughter Fatima.

Fustat The first Muslim city in Egypt, which was eventually absorbed into Cairo after the latter's foundation in 969.

haramayn 'The two sanctuaries'. Refers to Mecca and Medina.

hujja Lit. 'proof'. Shi'i literature uses the term to denote various signs or witnesses to God. The term was applied to key figures in Ismaili thought: the authoritative interpreters of the revelation of God, that is, the Imams; and as a reference to the chief *da'i*. The *hujja* was also a high rank in the Fatimid *da'wa*.

Ifriqiya The region that today comprises Tunisia and part of eastern Algeria. It was where the Fatimids first established their rule.

Ikhshidids Dynasty of Turkish governors who pledged nominal allegiance to the Abbasids.

ilm Knowledge. In Shi'i doctrine, every Imam possesses special knowledge (*ilm*), which is transmitted to him through *nass*.

Imam Generally used to denote a leader, whether a prayer leader or caliph. In Shi'i Islam, it refers to the designated Imams from the *ahl al-bayt*.

imamate The institution of authoritative political and religious leadership, which in Shi'i Islam refers to the designated Imams from the *ahl al-bayt*.

Ismailis Adherents of a branch of Shi'i Islam following the line of Isma'il, the eldest son of the Shi'i Imam Ja'far al-Sadiq (d. 765), from whom the Fatimid Imam-caliphs claimed descent.

Ithna'asharis Lit. 'Twelvers'; the majority branch of Shi'i Muslims who acknowledge 12 Imams in lineal succession from

Ali b. Abi Talib. After Imam Jaʿfar al-Sadiq, they acknowledged his younger son, Musa al-Kazim, as their Imam.

katib pl. *kuttab*   Secretary or scribe. While denoting any formal writer, in medieval Muslim contexts it denotes government officials and administrators.

Kutama   A significant Berber clan of the Sanhaja confederation of tribes. They served as the backbone of the Fatimid state in North Africa.

al-maghariba   'Westerners'. In Fatimid Egypt, the term was generally used to refer to Berber soldiers, officials, or Fatimid allies.

Maghrib   North Africa (present-day Morocco, Algeria, and Tunisia).

al-mahdi   Lit. 'the rightly guided one'; a term applied in Muslim eschatology to one who is the restorer of true religion and justice before the end of time. In Shiʿa Islam, the *mahdi* refers to a messianic Imam.

Mahdiyya   A coastal town in modern-day Tunisia, founded by the first Fatimid Imam-caliph, al-Mahdi bi'llah.

majalis   Lit. 'seating' or 'gathering'. As used by the Ismaili *daʿwa*, the term *majalis al-hikma* denoted the sessions where the believers received instruction on Ismaili beliefs.

Maliki   A Sunni school of law adhering
              to the teachings of Malik b. Anas
              (d. 795), with a significant presence
              in North Africa.

Mansuriyya   The second Fatimid city, founded
              by the Fatimid Imam-caliph
              al-Mansur bi'llah and located south
              of Qayrawan.

mashariqa   'Easterners'. In Fatimid Egypt, the
              term generally denoted Turkish
              soldiers or officials, but could
              include others of eastern origins
              such as Daylamis.

nass   Lit. 'text' or 'stipulation'. In Shi'i
              Islam, it refers to Prophet
              Muhammad's declaration of Ali as
              his successor and, by extension, of
              each Imam's appointment of his
              successor.

Nizaris   A branch of the Ismaili Shi'a who
              trace the imamate through Imam
              Nizar, the eldest son of the Fatimid
              Imam-caliph al-Mustansir.

Qahira   Cairo; city founded by the Fatimids
              in 969. It was named *al-Qahira
              al-Mu'izziya* (the Victorious City of
              al-Mu'izz) when al-Mu'izz took up
              residence there in 973.

Qaramita   A ninth-century Islamic revolution-
              ary movement following Hamdan
              Qarmat which, while adhering with
              the Ismailis to the imamate of
              Muhammad b. Isma'il b. Ja'far,

opposed the imamate of al-Mahdi bi'llah and the successive Fatimid Imam-caliphs.

Qayrawan — Tunisian city and the first Fatimid capital in 909; present-day Kairouan.

Seljuks — Turkish tribal dynasty that ruled parts of the Middle East and Asia Minor from 1037 to 1194.

Shafi'i — A Sunni school of law adhering to the teachings of Muhammad b. Idris al-Shafi'i (d. 820).

Sulayhids — An Ismaili dynasty in Yemen ruling from 1047 to 1138.

Tayyibi — A branch of the Ismaili Shi'a who trace the imamate through al-Musta'li, a son of the Fatimid Imam-caliph al-Mustansir, and thereafter through the Imam Tayyib, son of the Imam-caliph al-Amir.

Umayyads — First major ruling dynasty of Muslim history, based in Damascus (661–750); their successors ruled Andalusia from 711 to 1031.

Zirids — North-African Berber dynasty (972–1148) which ruled initially as Fatimid viceroys before declaring independence in the mid-11th century.

Notes

Chapter 1. The Arrival of the Fatimids in Egypt

1 On the origins, rise, and key developments of the Fatimid Empire in North Africa, see Shainool Jiwa, *The Fatimids: 1. The Rise of a Muslim Empire* (London, 2018).

2 al-Maqrizi, *Itti'az al-hunafa*, trans. Shainool Jiwa as *Towards a Shi'i Mediterranean Empire: Fatimid Egypt and the Founding of Cairo* (London, 2009), p. 71.

3 al-Maqrizi, *Shi'i Mediterranean Empire*, p. 77.

4 al-Maqrizi, *Shi'i Mediterranean Empire*, p. 104.

Chapter 2. The Genesis of Fatimid Rule in Egypt

1 al-Maqrizi, *Shi'i Mediterranean Empire*, pp. 107–8. Note: Asterisk (*) indicates square brackets in the original text.

2 al-Maqrizi, *Shi'i Mediterranean Empire*, pp. 212–13.

3 al-Maqrizi, *Itti'az al-hunafa*. Translation from Heinz Halm, *The Empire of the Mahdi: The Rise of the Fatimids*, trans. Michael Bonner (Leiden, 1996), p. 374.

4 Idris Imad al-Din, *Uyun al-akhbar*, trans. Shainool Jiwa as *The Founder of Cairo: The Fatimid Imam-Caliph al-Mu'izz and his Era* (London, 2013), p. 223.

5 al-Maqrizi, *Shi'i Mediterranean Empire*, p. 206.

6 al-Maqrizi, *Shi'i Mediterranean Empire*, p. 110.

7 al-Maqrizi, *Shi'i Mediterranean Empire*, p. 70.

8   al-Maqrizi, *Shi'i Mediterranean Empire*, p. 109.
9   al-Maqrizi, *Khitat*, as cited in al-Maqrizi, *Shi'i Mediterranean Empire*, p. 109, n.308.

Chapter 3. Towards an Inclusive Empire

1   al-Maqrizi, *Shi'i Mediterranean Empire*, p. 71.
2   al-Maqrizi, *Shi'i Mediterranean Empire*, p. 209.
3   Ibn Khallikan, *Wafayat al-a'yan*, trans. Mac Guckin de Slane as *Ibn Khallikan's Biographical Dictionary* (Paris, 1842–71), vol. 3, p. 526, citing al-Musabbihi.
4   Ibn Khallikan, *Biographical Dictionary*, vol. 3, p. 526.
5   al-Maqrizi, *Itti'az al-hunafa*, ed. Jamal al-Din al-Shayyal, 2nd ed. (Cairo, 1996), vol. 1, pp. 236–37.
6   Yahya b. Sa'id al-Antaki, *Histoire de Yahya-Ibn-Sa'id d'Antioche*, ed. Ignaty Kratchkovsky, French trans. Françoise Micheau and Gérard Troupeau in *Patrologia Orientalis* 23, no. 3 (1932), pp. 349–520, pp. 391–92.
7   al-Maqrizi, *Itti'az*, ed. Shayyal, vol. 3, p. 244.
8   Ibn Khallikan, *Biographical Dictionary*, vol. 4, p. 360.
9   al-Maqrizi, *Shi'i Mediterranean Empire*, pp. 113–14.
10 Ibn al-Athir, *al-Kamil fi'l-tarikh*, vol. 7, ed. Muhammad Yusuf al-Daqqaq (Beirut, 1987), p. 477. Similar reports are found, for example, in Ibn al-Jawzi, *al-Muntazam fi tarikh al-muluk wa'l-umam*, ed. Muhammad Abd al-Qadir Ata and Mustafa Abd al-Qadir Ata (Beirut, 1992), vol. 14, p. 386.
11 *Ta'rikh batarikat al-kanisa al-misriyya* (*History of the Patriarchs of the Coptic Church of Alexandria*), ed. and trans. Yassa Abd al-Masih, Aziz Suryal Atiya, Uswald Burmester, and Antoine Khater (Cairo, 1959–1968), vol. 2, p. 150.

Chapter 4. The Composition of the State

1 Nasir-i Khusraw, *Nāṣer-e Khosraw's Book of Travels (Safarnāma)*, trans. Wheeler M. Thackston, Jr (Albany, NY, 1986), pp. 45–47.

2 al-Maqrizi, *Itti'az*, ed. Shayyal, vol. 1, pp. 265–66.

3 al-Maqrizi, *Itti'az*, ed. Shayyal, vol. 1, p. 266.

4 al-Maqrizi, *Shi'i Mediterranean Empire*, p. 70.

5 al-Qadi al-Nu'man, *Kitab Ikhtilaf usul al-madhahib*, ed. and trans. Devin Stewart as *Disagreements of the Jurists: A Manual of Islamic Legal Theory* (New York, 2015), pp. 38–39.

6 Ibn Khallikan, *Biographical Dictionary*, vol. 3, p. 567.

7 al-Maqrizi, *al-Mawa'iz wa'l-i'tibar bi dhikr al-khitat wa'l-athar*, ed. Muhammad Zaynhum and Madihat al-Sharqawi (Cairo, 1996–98), vol. 2, p. 347.

8 Ibn Hawqal, *Kitab Surat al-Ard*, ed. J. H. Kramers (Leiden, 1938), vol. 1, pp. 147–48. This and the following extracts on the Qarafa mosque are translated in Jonathan M. Bloom, 'The Mosque of the Qarafa in Cairo', *Muqarnas* 4 (1987), pp. 7–20, p. 8.

9 al-Muqaddasi (al-Maqdisi), *Kitab Ahsan al-taqasim fi Ma'rifat al-aqalim*, ed. Michael Jan de Goeje, 2nd edition (Leiden, 1904), p. 209.

10 al-Maqrizi, *Khitat*, vol. 3, p. 326.

11 Ibn Khallikan, *Biographical Dictionary*, vol. 3, p. 529 (translation slightly modified).

12 Ibn al-Jawzi, *al-Muntazam*, in Paul E. Walker, ed. and trans., *Orations of the Fatimid Caliphs: Festival Sermons of the Ismaili Imams* (London, 2009), p. 141.

Chapter 5. Science and Scholarship in the City Victorious

1 al-Maqrizi, *Khitat*, translated in Heinz Halm, *The Fatimids and their Traditions of Learning* (London,

1997), p. 44. Asterisk indicates square brackets in the original text.

2 al-Maqrizi, *Khitat*, translated in Halm, *Traditions of Learning*, p. 45. Asterisks indicate square brackets in the original text.

3 al-Maqrizi, *Khitat*, translated in Halm, *Traditions of Learning*, pp. 73–74.

4 al-Maqrizi, *Khitat*, translated in Halm, *Traditions of Learning*, p. 76.

5 Ibn Khallikan, *Biographical Dictionary*, vol. 2, p. 365.

6 al-Nisaburi, *Risala al-mujaza al-kafiya fi adab al-du'at*, ed. and trans. Verena Klemm and Paul E. Walker as *A Code of Conduct: A Treatise on the Etiquette of the Fatimid Ismaili Mission* (London, 2011), pp. 47–49.

7 al-Kirmani, *al-Masabih fi ithbat al-imama*, ed. and trans. Paul E. Walker as *Master of the Age: An Islamic Treatise on the Necessity of the Imamate* (London, 2007), p. 126.

8 Ibn Khaldun, *Diwan al-mubtada wa'l-khabar fi tarikh al-arab wa'l-barbar*, ed. Khalil Shahadah and Suhayl Zakkar (Beirut, 2001), vol. 4, pp. 76–77.

9 Ibn Hammad (Hamadu), *Akhbar muluk bani ubayd*, ed. al-Tahami Naqrah and Abd al-Halim Uways (Cairo, 1981), p. 103.

Chapter 6. The Empire of the Seas

1 Yossef Rapoport and Emilie Savage-Smith, *Lost Maps of the Caliphs: Drawing the World in Eleventh-Century Cairo* (Chicago, IL, 2018).

2 Yossef Rapoport and Emilie Savage-Smith, ed. and trans., *An Eleventh-Century Egyptian Guide to the Universe: The Book of Curiosities* (Leiden, 2014), p. 488.

3   Rapoport and Savage-Smith, *Guide to the Universe*, p. 472.
4   Rapoport and Savage-Smith, *Guide to the Universe*, p. 473.
5   Yedida K. Stillmann and Paula Sanders, 'Ṭirāz', *Encyclopaedia of Islam, Second Edition*, ed. P. Bearman et al. First published online, 2012. http://dx.doi.org.iij.idm.oclc.org/10.1163/1573-3912_islam_COM_1228
6   Idris Imad al-Din, *The Founder of Cairo*, p. 200.
7   The Aga Khan, 'Inaugural Ceremony of the Delegation of the Ismaili Imamat, Ottawa' (speech, Ottawa, 6 December 2008). Transcript at https://www.akdn.org/speech/his-highness-aga-khan/inaugural-ceremony-delegation-ismaili-imamat-ottawa

Chapter 7. The Fluctuations of Fatimid Rule

1   Ibn Muyassar, *Akhbar Misr*, ed. Ayman F. Sayyid (Cairo, 1981), p. 25, cited in Delia Cortese and Simonetta Calderini, *Women and the Fatimids in the World of Islam* (Edinburgh, 2006), p. 110.
2   Verena Klemm, *Memoirs of a Mission: The Ismaili Scholar, Statesman and Poet al-Mu'ayyad fi'l-Din al-Shirazi* (London, 2003), p. 72.
3   al-Shirazi, *al-Majalis al-Mu'ayyadiya*, vols 1–2, ed. Hatim Hamid al-Din (Bombay, 1975–1986), vols. 1 and 3, ed. Mustafa Ghalib (Beirut, 1974–84).
4   Nasir-i Khusraw, *Book of Travels*, p. 2.
5   Annemarie Schimmel, trans. and intro., *Make a Shield from Wisdom: Selected Verses from Nāṣir-i Khusraw's* Dīvān (London, 2001), p. 47.
6   Nasir-i Khusraw, *Forty Poems from the Divan*, intro. and trans. Peter L. Wilson and Gholam Reza Aavani (Tehran, 1977), p. 8.

7 Eric Ormsby, *Between Reason and Revelation: Twin Wisdoms Reconciled* (London, 2012), p. 4.

8 Nasir-i Khusraw, *Book of Travels*, pp. 62–63.

9 The single surviving copy of this coin is part of the collection of the Institute of Ismaili Studies. For further details see https://www.iis.ac.uk/gallery/nizar-b-al-mustansir-bi-llah-gold-dinar

Chapter 8. Late Fatimid Egypt and the Heirs of Empire

1 August C. Krey, *The First Crusade: The Accounts of Eyewitnesses and Participants* (Princeton, NJ, 1921), 256–57.

2 Krey, *The First Crusade*, p. 262.

3 Ibn Khallikan, *Biographical Dictionary*, vol. 1, p. 614.

4 Ibn Muyassar, *Akhbar Misr*, p. 101.

5 Ibn Jubayr, *Travels*, p. 37, as cited in Caroline Williams, 'The Cult of ʿAlid Saints in the Fatimid Monuments of Cairo. Part II: The Mausolea', *Muqarnas* 3 (1985), pp. 39–60, p. 53.

6 al-Maqrizi, *Shiʿi Mediterranean Empire*, p. 112.

7 al-Maqrizi, *Khitat*, vol. 2, p. 119.

8 al-Maqrizi, *Khitat*, vol. 2, p. 119.

Conclusion. Glimpses of the Fatimid Legacy

1 al-Maqrizi, *Shiʿi Mediterranean Empire*, p. 104.

2 The Aga Khan, 'Inauguration of al-Azhar Park' (speech, Cairo, 25 March 2005). Transcript at https://www.akdn.org/speech/his-highness-aga-khan/inauguration-al-azhar-park

Further Reading

Fatimid studies continues to be a burgeoning field of scholarship. For an extended survey that integrates the Fatimids within the broader canvas of Ismaili history and thought, from their formation to the present day, Farhad Daftary's *The Isma'ilis: Their History and Doctrines* (2nd edition, Cambridge, 2007), pp. 137–295, remains paramount. Daftary's more recent work, *The Ismaili Imams: A Biographical History* (London, 2020), includes biographical surveys of the lives of the Fatimid Imam-caliphs from al-Mahdi bi'llah to al-Mustansir and Nizar. Paul Walker's *Exploring an Islamic Empire: Fatimid History and its Sources* (London, 2002), pp. 15–91, provides a summative account of the Fatimid period, followed by a critical evaluation of the sources on Fatimid history. A succinct account of the Egyptian era of Fatimid history is also found in Paula Sanders's 'The Fatimid State, 969–1171', in *The Cambridge History of Egypt, volume 1: Islamic Egypt, 640–1517*, ed. Carl F. Petry (Cambridge, 1998), pp. 151–74. Heinz Halm's entry on the Fatimids in the *Encyclopaedia of Islam* (3rd edition) provides a brief but important overview, and now supersedes those of earlier editions.

Detailed studies and monographs on diverse aspects of Fatimid history are plentiful. Most comprehensive in scope is Heinz Halm's three-volume series (in German). While volume one, *Das Reich das Mahdi: Der Aufstieg der Fatimiden* (Munich, 1991) focusses principally on the Fatimids in Ifriqiya, it concludes with the Fatimid entry into Egypt. *Das Reich* has been translated into English by Michael Bonner as *The Empire of the Mahdi: The Rise of the Fatimids* (Leiden, 1996). Halm's subsequent volumes, *Die Kalifen von Kairo: Die Fatimiden in Ägypten, 973–1073* (Munich, 2003) and *Kalifen und Assassinen: Ägypten und der Vordere Orient zur Zeit der ersten Kreuzzüge, 1074–1171* (Munich, 2014), provide detailed coverage of the Egyptian phase. The principal contemporary study of Fatimid history in the Arabic language remains Ayman Fu'ad Sayyid's *Al-Dawla al-Fatimiyya fi Misr: Tafsir jadid* (2nd edition, Cairo, 2000). Michael Brett's *The Fatimid Empire* (Edinburgh, 2017) provides an excellent handbook on Fatimid history. Amongst the wide range of subject-specific works on Fatimid history, Paul Walker's *Caliph of Cairo: Al-Hakim bi-Amr Allah 996–1021* (Cairo, 2012) charts the most detailed study of al-Hakim's reign to date. Delia Cortese and Simonetta Calderini's *Women and the Fatimids in the World of Islam* (Edinburgh, 2006) remains central for elucidating the role and impact of women in the Fatimid age.

Since the publication of volume 1 of this work, a swathe of new studies on Fatimid history has continued to invigorate the field. Particularly important is Yossef Rapoport and Emilie Savage-Smith's *Lost Maps of the Caliphs: Drawing the World in Eleventh-Century Cairo* (Chicago and London, 2018) for its ground-breaking analysis of the *Kitab Ghara'ib al-funun*, based on their 2014 translation. The study of the corpus of *geniza* fragments from the Ben Ezra synagogue has in recent years become a major field of research. Through a detailed investigation of the fragments, Marina Rustow's *The Lost Archive: Traces of a Caliphate in a Cairo Synagogue* (Princeton, NJ, 2020) painstakingly reconstructs Fatimid archival practices while also signifying a major reconsideration of the nature of state-hood in the medieval Muslim world.

* * *

Select Reading List

Brett, Michael. *The Fatimid Empire*. Edinburgh, 2017.

Cortese, Delia, and Simonetta Calderini. *Women and the Fatimids in the World of Islam*. Edinburgh, 2006.

Daftary, Farhad. *The Isma'ilis: Their History and Doctrines*. 2nd ed., Cambridge, 2007.

——. *The Ismaili Imams: A Biographical History*. London, 2020.

Halm, Heinz. *The Empire of the Mahdi*, trans. M. Bonner. Leiden, 1996.

——. *The Fatimids and their Traditions of Learning.* London, 1997.

Jiwa, Shainool, trans. *Towards a Shi'i Mediterranean Empire: Fatimid Egypt and the Founding of Cairo. The Reign of the Imam-caliph al-Mu'izz from al-Maqrizi's* Itti'az al-Hunafa. London, 2009.

——. *The Founder of Cairo: The Fatimid Imam-caliph al-Mu'izz and His Era. An English translation of the text on al-Mu'izz from Idris Imad al-Din's* Uyun al-Akhbar. London, 2013.

Rapoport, Yossef, and Emilie Savage-Smith, ed. and trans. *An Eleventh-Century Egyptian Guide to the Universe: The Book of Curiosities.* Leiden, 2014.

——. *Lost Maps of the Caliphs: Drawing the World in Eleventh-Century Cairo.* Chicago and London, 2018.

Rustow, Marina. *The Lost Archive: Traces of a Caliphate in a Cairo Synagogue.* Princeton, NJ, 2020.

Walker, Paul E. *Exploring an Islamic Empire: Fatimid History and its Sources.* London, 2002.

——. *Caliph of Cairo: Al-Hakim bi-Amr Allah 996–1021.* Cairo, 2012.

List of Illustrations

Index

Bold is used for Fatimid Imam-caliphs. *Italic* text is used for Arabic terms and titles. *Italic* numbers are used for illustrations. Places are in Egypt unless shown otherwise and modern countries are used.

World of Islam Series

The *World of Islam* series aims to provide non-specialist readers with a reliable and balanced overview of the diverse manifestations of Islam. It seeks to redress misperceptions by offering a nuanced survey of the plurality of interpretations amongst Muslims around the world and throughout history, who express their faith and values through varied cultural, social, intellectual and religious means. Covering themes pertinent to Muslims and non-Muslims alike, the civilizational series approach encourages readers to delve into the commonalities as well as the distinctions that define different Muslim traditions. In accessible language and concise format, these books deliver well-researched yet easy-to-follow introductions that will stimulate readers to think differently about Islam.

Be inspired by the World of Islam.

The Institute of Ismaili Studies

The Institute of Ismaili Studies was established in 1977 with the object of promoting scholarship and learning on Islam, in the historical as well as contemporary contexts, and a better understanding of its relationship with other societies and faiths.

The Institute's programmes encourage a perspective which is not confined to the theological and religious heritage of Islam, but seeks to explore the relationship of religious ideas to broader dimensions of society and culture. The programmes thus encourage an interdisciplinary approach to the materials of Islamic history and thought. Particular attention is also given to issues of modernity that arise as Muslims seek to relate their heritage to the contemporary situation.

Within the Islamic tradition, the Institute's programmes promote research on those areas which have, to date, received relatively little attention from scholars. These include the intellectual and literary expressions of Shi'ism in general, and Ismailism in particular.

In the context of Islamic societies, the Institute's programmes are informed by the full range and diversity of cultures in which Islam is practised today, from the Middle East, South and Central Asia, and Africa to the industrialized societies of the West, thus taking into consideration the variety of contexts which shape the ideals, beliefs and practices of the faith.

These objectives are realised through concrete programmes and activities organized and implemented by various departments of the Institute. The Institute also collaborates periodically, on a programme-specific basis, with other institutions of learning in the United Kingdom and abroad.

In facilitating publications, the Institute's sole aim is to encourage original research and analysis of relevant issues. While every effort is made to ensure that the publications are of a high standard, there is naturally bound to be a diversity of views, ideas and interpretations. As such, the opinions expressed in these publications must be understood as belonging to their authors alone.